# Praise for Lomas Brown and
## *If These Walls Could Talk: Detroit Lions*

**Wayne Fontes (former Lions head coach)**: "If you don't like Lomas Brown, you don't like apple pie and America."

**Bill Muir (former Lions offensive line coach)**: "It's his personality, his attitude. There's a humility about him. It's not a lack of confidence, he just never flaunted who he was, what he did. Lomas is always respectful. I just radiate to people who are reliable, accountable, and you can put a capital in front of all those words for Lomas. I knew what he was going to be like every single day. You deal with players, and they're different every day. There's no standard level of performance for every day. I love that about Lomas. Not an ordinary level, either. I know everything in his career wasn't easy, but he persevered until he had it done. That in a nutshell is him. If he called today, I would drop whatever I was doing."

**Jay Crawford (former co-worker at ESPN)**: "I always used to joke that, have you ever had a bad day? Are you ever in a bad mood? His smile is electric, and it's always ready. His laugh is one of the most contagious laughs I've ever been around. I just think that of all the people I've ever met—not just athletes—there's just not many like him, who seem to just light up the room with their energy and their laughter, their energy, their demeanor... I'm glad to call him one of my friends and I'm proud and very lucky to work with him as long as I did."

**Chris Spielman (former Lions linebacker)**: "His off-the-field personality and gentleness is special, not to mention his smile. I think of him often, and he's got the genuine smile, really a gentle giant. He was an intense guy on gameday, but I always admired him because he could be such a mean SOB on the field but turn that off after the game was over. Let's just say I'm glad I was always on his team. I'm not surprised that he could do that because you saw that in his genuine smile and personality. The fact that he's an All-Pro offensive tackle, well, you can't be a nice guy doing that. Off the field is a different story."

**Bill Keenist (Detroit Lions senior vice president, communications)**: "He's genuine, he's real, appreciates the same in people. He's just the kind of guy that everyone would love to call a friend. He's been that way since Day One with me. He's a teddy bear, but on the football field, he was exceptional."

**Mike Utley (former Lions offensive lineman)**: "I have nothing but good things to say about Lomas 'Big Daddy' Brown. I really enjoy him and his wife, Wendy. The other day, we were busting chops back and forth, and my wife couldn't believe it. I told her that's male bonding. If I didn't have respect for Lomas and he for me, none of this would happen. You find an opening, rub a little rock salt into it. It makes you a better ballplayer, a better teammate, a better friend. Over the years, Lomas has become a better friend. It's a privilege that he calls me his friend."

**Rob Rubick (former Lions tight end):** "You always hear about the 'great locker room guy,' but Lomas truly was. He was always pleasant, never negative toward the team. He just came in always ready to work, happy. When we were losing, he wasn't one jumping off the bandwagon. He was always going to come and do his job. You hear all these clichés, but the clichés are true for a reason. I guarantee you by his 18th year in the league, everyone in the locker room was looking to him. He had done it all, he'd seen the ups and downs of a season; he knew it was a marathon, not a sprint. The NFL is a grind, and he just had that perfect demeanor to handle that grind."

**Dana Jacobson (former co-worker at ESPN):** "I had met Lomas 10 years earlier, while working in Detroit. He came in at ESPN, and this teddy bear of a man I remembered engulfed me in a hug, knowing I was a Lions fan…I could tell he was such a gentle giant, a genuinely good soul. He wanted me to know he cared enough to remember. Just hearing him say 'D'—he always called me 'D'—brought a smile to my face…That's the thing, to know Lomas is to love Lomas. A fierce football player but again a teddy bear of a man."

**Rob Parker (former co-worker at ESPN, longtime media personality in Detroit):** "I've had many people, from all walks of life, stop me and say, 'I love that man. He's the best.' They felt compelled to spread the word about Lomas' appeal. And as someone who has known Lomas since I first arrived in Detroit in 1993, I understand it. The term 'great guy' is grossly overused. Here, with Lomas Brown, it fits perfectly."

# *If These*
# WALLS
# *Could* TALK:
## DETROIT LIONS

# *If These* **WALLS**
# *Could* **TALK:**
## DETROIT LIONS

## Stories from the Detroit Lions Sideline, Locker Room, and Press Box

Lomas Brown with Mike Isenberg

## TRIUMPH
### BOOKS

Library of Congress Cataloging-in-Publication Data
Names: Brown, Lomas | Isenberg, Mike
Title: If these walls could talk : Detroit Lions : stories from the Detroit
   Lions sideline, locker room, and press box / by Lomas Brown, with Mike
   Isenberg.
Description: Chicago, Illinois : Triumph Books LLC, [2016]
Identifiers: LCCN 2016004703 | ISBN 9781629371580
Subjects: LCSH: Detroit Lions (Football team)—Anecdotes. | Detroit Lions
   (Football team)—History.
Classification: LCC GV956.D4 .B76 2016 | DDC 796.332/640977434—dc23
LC record available at https://lccn.loc.gov/2016004703

This book is available in quantity at special discounts for your group or organization. For further information, contact:

Triumph Books LLC
814 North Franklin Street
Chicago, Illinois 60610
(312) 337-0747
www.triumphbooks.com

Printed in U.S.A.

ISBN: 978-1-62937-158-0

Design by Amy Carter

Photos courtesy of USA TODAY Sports Images unless otherwise indicated

*I'd like to thank my wife, Wendy, aka Girly; behind every man's good accomplishments is a great woman, and she was behind me every step of the way. One of the best aspects of retiring from the game is that I get to spend more time with her.*

*My children mean more to me than I can put into words. I love y'all (Antoinette, Ashley, Adrienne, Trey, Jayla).*

*Finally, the NFL was always teased as "Not For Long." To play 18 years with the many guys and personalities and to savor the many memories and experiences that I still enjoy today makes me know I am truly blessed!*
*—Lomas Brown*

*This is dedicated to my children, Zachary and Alexandra (Cookie), who have taught me about unconditional love, and my wife, Katie, who helped me learn how to love and be loved. You three are the highlight of my life and my inspiration. Thanks for all of your support and encouragement.*
*—Mike Isenberg*

# CONTENTS

# FOREWORD

I first met Lomas Brown just before my rookie season in the NFL in 1989. Today, more than 25 years later, I consider him not just a teammate, not just a friend, but a brother.

I came to the Lions as a 21-year-old country boy from Wichita, Kansas. Detroit seemed like the biggest place in the world to me. You see a lot of young players in all sports get caught up in the wrong crowd or make bad decisions. Lomas made sure this never happened to me.

I was at his home so often, I probably should have paid rent. With all the craziness happening on the field, spending time with his wife and kids gave me a safe place to relax.

Even though Lomas was only a couple of years older than me, he had already experienced the highs and lows of the NFL. He was so savvy to the business side of the league and made sure he protected me. His counsel in that regard was priceless.

And oh yes, he was also a Hall of Fame-level left tackle. The way that he and guys like Kevin Glover took care of me on the field made it easy to work hard for them. I never wanted to let those guys down. He's really just an all-around great guy, very likable, and he has one of those personalities that just meshes with everyone in any situation. Those are people that you want to see succeed, and he definitely did. What's most impressive to me is that not only did he do great things, but he's never stopped appreciating the opportunities he's received.

It was an honor to play with Lomas and it's an even bigger one to call him my brother.

*—Barry Sanders*

Courtesy Detroit Lions

# INTRODUCTION

When Mike Isenberg first approached me with this project, I was skeptical. *Is my story that interesting? Would people actually care what I have to say?* Even after a few conversations, I still wasn't sold. The more we spoke, though, the more my interest started to pique. Playing 18 years in the NFL, I was fortunate to have experienced just about everything. There was good, there was bad, and there was just crazy.

My 11 years with the Lions had both triumph and tragedy. We rose from nothing and were *so* close to bringing the city of Detroit the winner they so deserve. There may not have been any Super Bowls, but that was the basis of friendships that I still hold dear today. I spent three years in Arizona. That was just pure craziness. You know how kids like to text "SMH" for shaking my head? That sums up the Cardinals years.

After a forgettable year in Cleveland, I thought my career was over. But the next season, I was starting in the Super Bowl for the New York Giants. I had finally made it to the big game. Unfortunately, we got crushed by the Baltimore Ravens, and two years later, I was *positive* that my career was done—until I came home to give it one more shot with the Tampa Bay Buccaneers. In my last game, I finally was a champion.

But the focus of this book is on the Lions. I was fortunate to play with some great players like Jerry Ball, Kevin Glover, Herman Moore, Chris Spielman, and, of course, the incomparable Barry Sanders. I've shared stories on all of them, along with the ups and downs of my time with the Lions, including our problems finding a quarterback, reaching the NFC Championship Game in 1991, and Mike Utley's awful injury. Never one to shy away from an opinion, you'll also read my take on the modern day Lions and guys like Matthew Stafford and Calvin Johnson.

My story isn't really about the destination; it's about the journey. As a boy, I never thought about football. I was more concerned with playing the trombone. From growing up in Miami during the tumultuous 1970s to the whole recruiting battles and learning about the life of a football player, I've had a charmed life. I'm glad Mike talked me into sharing my stories. I hope you enjoy it.

# Chapter 1
## Barry Sanders

It's the question I probably get more than any other: is Barry Sanders the best running back in NFL history? The only way I can answer is that Barry is the best I've ever seen. I know a lot of older folks swear by Jim Brown—when you look at his numbers, it's hard to argue—but Barry was unreal from Day One and never slowed down.

When the Lions thought about drafting Barry, it wasn't the no-brainer that it eventually turned out to be. Sure, he won the Heisman Trophy at Oklahoma State, but he was still kind of a mystery. At that time period, not every game was televised, and even though we all kept reading about this incredible back, not many of us had seen him play.

**Wayne Fontes (Lions head coach):** "That year there was a tremendous amount of great No. 1 draft picks. That was the year Dallas picked Troy Aikman right before us. Green Bay took Tony Mandarich, an offensive tackle. We had the third pick, and I remember going to Oklahoma State to watch Barry work out and I watched all 11 of his game films, and there was no question about it. He was the best player for us. When he came into the locker room, he was loved by the players, and, of course, Lomas liked him."

Barry showed up, and the first thing that hit me was how small this dude was. I'm talking about his height because he was rock solid. His thighs were so thick that you couldn't help but stare at them. As we got practicing, it was as clear as day that Barry was special. He went all-out every single play. A lot of running backs would slow down either at the end of a play or the end of practice. Not him. He had a way of visualizing how he'd play in the games and he wasn't slowing down there. He'd go another 30 to 40 yards.

**Bill Muir (Lions offensive line coach)**: "I have a saying that the high tide rises all boats in the harbor. What happens when you get a unique talent like Barry Sanders? Everyone's level of proficiency rises. The way he improvised, you couldn't anticipate. As an offensive lineman, you learn that the play is never over. What you do is you extend yourself, play with more of a positive attitude, and know that he's going to make something out of nothing. Let's just stay with block. That kind of contagiousness he brought to the team."

**Mike Utley (Lions offensive lineman)**: "How do you block for Barry Sanders? You stay out of his way!"

**Kevin Glover (Lions center)**: "It wasn't a challenge in a negative way for me. The challenge was to be in great shape and to keep moving forward. A lot of times plays are two to three seconds long, but with a great player like Barry, it's eight to 10 seconds. So the challenge was to get everyone to understand that when you think the play is over, it's not. You need to keep on going. You might have missed your block, but that person isn't going to get Barry down one-on-one."

**Fontes**: "Lomas came to me one time and said, 'Coach, when you call this play this 19 straight play, the fellas on the line, we're not sure which way to block our guys.' I said, 'Lomas, put a hat on the guy, and let Barry decide which way he wants to run.'"

Once the games started, nothing could stop him. Even when we ran the run-and-shoot, which is not a sound offense for quarterbacks

Barry Sanders was not only the best back to ever play, but he was also a true class act. (Courtesy Detroit Lions)

or backs because there was nobody left to block, it worked for us because of Barry. He was a walking time bomb. You just never knew when he was going to go off. It was like watching Barry Bonds. You never wanted to miss an at-bat because you never knew when Bonds was going to go deep.

When Sanders came to Detroit, he was just a country boy who was on his own for really the first time. I was going into my fourth year in the league and had already experienced the highs and—especially with the Lions at that time—a lot of lows. It was obvious that he was the future of the franchise, but he needed leadership. My job was not only to protect him *on* the field, but off of it as well.

Let me say that this wasn't just with Barry but all of the younger guys. As a leader of the team, I wanted them to come in and I'd try to make them comfortable. You want to try and protect them from some of the pitfalls out there—the pariahs, who want their time and their money. You try to protect them as much as you can. Being a professional is totally different than college. Back then everything was taken care of for you. From eating to your living arrangements to getting your parents tickets to the game, it was all good. But in the NFL, it all falls on you. That's the biggest thing I see in the pros with guys that get out there and either don't last long or don't make it. Some of it is their ability on the field, but a lot of it is their ability to handle things off the field. You're going to have all kinds of things come up off the field. That's life, and you aren't going to stop life from happening, but you've got to be able to separate the two. When you're at the facility, you've got to be able to concentrate and do your job and do it at the highest level. And that's not just in the game. That's practice; it's every day out there.

I wanted to show Barry that he had support. And it wasn't just Barry; it was his family, too. You need to ingratiate yourself with the family and let the family feel comfortable. That's what we did. I wouldn't say it was just myself, but our teams in the late '80s and '90s had a true family atmosphere. We'd hang out with the guys, we'd socialize. Guys wouldn't just go their separate ways. Barry could come over to my house any time he wanted to, to Kevin Glover's house, and it was the same way with any player. I think that's why in the '90s we had so much success.

And Barry was part of my family. One of the funniest parts of this was how my daughters looked at him. They were pretty young at the time and weren't really into football. Yet, here they were, hanging out with the best running back in the NFL. Part of why they got along so well was because Barry was about the same height as they were! And they didn't care about his record-breaking stats. They enjoyed being with the Barry that other people never saw— the giggling Barry, the Barry that *tried* to crack jokes. They just fell in love with him. For me, getting to know what type of person he is made me want to block even harder for him.

I always get people asking, "What is something nobody knows about Barry?" Well, let me say, this boy can eat! My ex-wife was a great cook, and she loved doing it. Barry made sure that none of it went to waste either. I have no idea where he put it all, but this shy, little guy from Kansas was over to our house *every* night!

Me and Glove knew that Barry was our ticket. All of the sudden, we were getting on *Monday Night Football*. Everyone wanted to see him. We started a rule that Barry would never have to pick himself up off the ground. This guy was working so hard on every play, that the least we could do was show appreciation by helping him up. We also knew that by doing that we could make sure there was no extracurricular activity. Barry carried so much of the load for us, and we appreciated it.

**Chris Spielman (Lions linebacker)**: "Well, these guys knew where their paycheck was coming from. Barry had so much energy on his runs. Me, I never helped a guy up. Not to be a tough guy, but I wanted him to exert as much energy as possible during a game. I don't think there's a more respected guy than Barry. Our guys loved him more than anyone. If I was a coach, I'd make sure those guys got their asses down the field to help him up too!"

**Barry Sanders (Lions running back)**: "That meant everything. I knew that those guys were looking out for me and I was playing for a group of guys, especially Lomas and Glove who wanted to see me do well. And it really mattered to them, and they took it to heart. They really did. For me it made me all the more hungry to extend myself. In the NFL everyone around you is not always pulling for you, but for those guys I always knew I was taking the field with guys who really wanted to see me succeed...I certainly did not want to let them down. It felt like we had a unique thing at that time. Almost like every other relationship, you respect the other party. I certainly didn't want to let those guys down."

**Fontes**: "We'd leave the field after everyone was done running and we'd be going to lunch or something, and Barry Sanders would be running by himself. He knew he had to run more because in practice, when Lomas and those guys were banging and banging and banging, I never allowed anyone to bump Barry. He was untouchable in practice. So I'd tell Lomas we were going to give the ball to Barry on this play in practice, so make sure you tell the defensive guys that Barry was going to get it, so leave the hole open, and let him run through it. There would be no tackling Barry Sanders. So Lomas would break the huddle, get up to the line, and he'd tell a Chris Spielman or a Jerry Ball, 'Hey, let us open a hole, and let Barry run through it.' Then he'd turn to me, and say, 'Coach, the fellas say they're going to knock Barry sideways!' Then we'd run the play, and nobody would touch Barry. Lomas controlled everything. But they respected that. Lomas told all the rookies, do not touch this guy, he needs to have a clean jersey, or we're all in trouble."

But what really struck me was the class he always displayed. He never pointed out anyone missing a block or making a bad play. Never. We'd run through a wall for that guy.

As spectacular as Barry was on the field, off of it he was just Barry. Just as my outspoken personality complemented Glove, it was the same way with Barry. Especially during his first few years in the league, Barry would come by my house and hang out with the family. He was single at the time, so I think it made him feel closer to home. He'd come over to my house every holiday and he was always dropping by to play with the kids, but Barry never really hung out with us players. He didn't drink, so clubs weren't really an option. But he was cool. We'd talk about social matters, about his crush on Olympic star Gail Devers. It was just friends talking together. He had a golf tournament ever year and was a great family man.

**Sanders**: "As far as Lomas, let me tell you about our relationship. Coming in as a rookie, I'm still college-aged because I left as a junior. We didn't live that far apart, and for some reason, some way, somehow, we just ended up at his home a lot. I don't remember specific details, but I remember that I ended up at his home quite often; it was almost like a second home. He had young kids at that point, and I would spend hours over there. For me, it was kind of a refuge. For Lomas, it must have been hectic with him being a young man himself in the NFL, being married, having kids, and those responsibilities.

"I spent a lot of time over there, even some Thanksgiving dinners. Throughout the seasons, whether it was to get a home-cooked meal or just to spend some time talking to Lomas, I grew up in a big family, and in a certain sense, it was home for me. I'm pretty sure I wore out my welcome. Haha. But I never got that sense from him. His daughters seemed to be amused and enjoyed it as well, and that's pretty much what it was. We'd talk about different things."

You could say that I was the yin to Barry's yang. You had one guy who likes (okay, loves) to talk and another who doesn't say anything. It was like the odd couple.

**Sanders**: "If that's what they say, I guess that's fine. There's a lot of truth to that. When I first got here, he definitely carried me for a lot of years away from the field, giving a young man someplace constructive to go, where I felt almost at home. I could have been a lot of other places as a young player, but oftentimes I'd be at his house. As boring as that sounds, it was a place of refuge. When you're in a big city, there are other things you could have been doing, so I'm glad the door was open, and that's where I was."

Sanders was always linked with the other great runner of that era, Emmitt Smith. There were definitely similarities and stark differences at the same time. The popular thinking is that if Barry played behind the massive Dallas offensive line, he'd have gained a ton more yards. I will disagree. Sure, the Cowboys had studs like Larry Allen and Nate Newton, but we did have two All-Pros as well. That's a pet peeve for me.

Playing so many years with Barry, of course I'm biased, but me and Emmitt are fraternity brothers, so we're tight too. Both guys have the best balance I've ever seen from a running back. It ain't easy getting either one down. They were both super-competitive, too. You can tell they knew this was a gift, and they worked really hard to not waste it.

Emmitt was more of a north and south runner, while Barry was faster and more elusive. Nobody had the vision of Emmitt, waiting to set up his blocks. Smith probably had more power, but Barry was the best at improvising while looking for the home run. I admire both guys because they were football players. They were no-frills guys who were just doing their job.

**Utley**: "It was 1990. I had just got done training, recovering from my broken leg. I was the only one in the locker room, and Barry opens the door and comes walking in. I said, 'Barr, I have a question for you.' He bent down, picks up a football, and starts walking toward me. I go, 'Barr, I've got to ask you a question. Why don't you spike the football?' And he started twirling the ball, walking toward me, and he tossed it to me, and said, 'I expected to be there.' And he walked into the training room. Now that is a man with class."

While Barry's excellence challenged us as players, it was also critical for our coaches to know the best way to utilize this once-in-a-lifetime weapon.

**Glover**: "He might have 20 yards at halftime, but don't give up on the running game, keep feeding him the ball. The last year we played together, Sylvester Croom was the offensive coordinator, and Bobby Ross was the head coach...After the first two games, Barry had only 53 yards, and I had a talk with Coach Ross, and he spoke to Coach Croom, and they understood...we have the best runner in the history of the game, so keep feeding him the ball, and good things will happen. Fortunately, they listened."

Sanders ended up with 2,053 yards rushing, so he actually ran for 2,000 yards in just 14 games, an amazing accomplishment.

Barry's biggest fan and toughest critic was his father. William Sanders was as old school as you get. I know how proud he was of his son, but he never wavered in saying that Jim Brown was the best running back in NFL history. Mr. Sanders never gave many compliments. It was something I can relate to.

In my entire life, I can only remember my father complimenting me twice. Once was in college, which I don't remember the specific circumstances, and the other was with the New York Giants. I had a really good game against Hugh Douglas of the Philadelphia Eagles, and John Madden was pumping me up all game. Afterward, Dad called and said, "Now they saw the game. Now they know the name!" I was stunned. I always knew what my father meant to me, and Barry was the same way.

\* \* \*

If you ever want to get my blood boiling, go ahead and criticize Barry Sanders for walking away from the game. People that say that have no idea what they're talking about.

The year after he broke the 2,000-yard mark, Barry followed it up with another 1,491. He was 30 years old and was just 1,457 yards away from Walter Payton's NFL record. Nobody thought he was ready to retire.

But Barry has never been about what people think and certainly not about records. In his rookie year, he was trailing Christian Okoye of the Kansas City Chiefs by 10 yards for the rushing title. Yet, he pulled himself out of the game because it wasn't important to him. I've seen him turn down commercials that would pay him $250,000 just to stand there! Let's be honest, if Barry wanted to play a few more years, that all-time rushing record would be so far out of reach that nobody would have caught him. But he stayed true to his convictions and walked away.

**Glover:** "I came back for his last game against the Ravens...we sat in the locker room for a long time. I kind of had a feeling that day [that it was his last game]...I know he didn't give a hoot about records and accomplishments. It was all about his commitment to the team and love for the game. As a professional athlete, when the desire to prepare isn't the same, it's time to move on."

I sometimes think about what would have happened had Glove, Chris Spielman, Jerry Ball, and myself stuck around in Detroit. Would Barry have still retired when he did?

**Sanders**: "I don't know. You just never know. I know that they did so much for the organization as men. You can't replace them with another jersey number or another guy. Good teams were able to balance that. As far as me continuing to play, I'm not sure."

When Barry went into the Hall of Fame, he said he didn't choose football, football chose him. I think that is so fitting for him. If you think about it, here's this man in the brutal sport we play, playing one of the most demanding positions. He gave Michigan the best 10 years an individual ever had here. He gave it everything he had. Nobody would ever say that he slacked off. The games were the easy part. It's the preparation, the lifting, the treatments. You get used to that, but the mental aspect is even tougher.

I don't think Barry really wanted to play football, but his talents were so great that he couldn't be denied. All of these "experts" say he should have given more. Let me tell you something: in this sport any game can be your last. He could have been another Mike Utley. A guy like Barry should be able to leave on any terms he wants.

Barry pretty much kept to himself. He was cordial enough with the team, but you never saw him out and about. That's why I'm so surprised to see his profile getting so much bigger since his retirement. I think it's great for him to get himself out there. People should see what type of guy he is, and hey, if he wants to make a little money with different projects, more power to him. Selfishly, I'm hoping that maybe his visibility might help me get into the Hall of Fame. After all, as great as he was, Barry would be the first to tell you he didn't get all of those yards himself.

There's one more thing about Barry that most people don't know. Sure, when he was playing, Barry was the king of the two or three-word answers. His standard response to questions was, "Is that right?" But here's the truth—the guy thinks he's a comedian! The thing is that he gets his digs in quietly. We'd get on him, though, about how he always wore tight clothes, and the fact that the best running back of his era was still driving an old Acura into his sixth year in the NFL. And believe me, Barry gives it right back.

# Chapter 2

# My Early Years
# with the Lions

**M**y adjustments to the NFL were pretty eye-opening. Aside from the weather, the money and everything else, the Lions were a whole lot different than my Florida Gators.

My first coach was Darryl Rogers. He has a reputation for being tightly wound, but I never really saw that side of him. I didn't know much about him, other than he won a Big Ten title at Michigan State with a wide receiver (and future Detroit Tigers star) Kirk Gibson. Overall, I just thought he was a nice man, but that doesn't mean he didn't have his quirks.

We were rookies at the same time, and the team clearly had big expectations for both of us. I was starting at left tackle on the first day. I always thought he did a nice job of keeping the pressure off of me in games—and in practice.

**Wayne Fontes (Lions defensive coordinator):** "We had a pass drill, and I was there watching one of our defensive stalwarts, who was an All-Pro at the time. Lomas lined up against him. The player says, 'Okay, rookie, I'm going to show you how it is in the NFL.' Darryl Rogers says hike, and the defensive player tried to use the over/under swim move. Lomas stood back and just stopped him in his tracks. Everybody on the offense went wild, and started yelling, 'Lo-mas, Lo-mas!' The big fellah had a big smile on his face and just stuffed the guy. He had nothing but a big smile."

**Chris Spielman (Lions linebacker):** "I will say this, though, I don't think Lomas was the greatest practice player. I remember once he got beat in a one-on-one drill, and the guy who beat him was talking some smack. Lomas just said, 'Let's run it again.' He then picked the guy up and slammed him to the ground. That's why I always wanted to be on his side. If he could take a big defensive lineman and throw him like a rag doll, I wanted to be on his side. That is what I remember the most about him. Man was he good. But on Sundays, not Wednesdays."

One day, Coach Rogers was standing off to the side as we all practiced. This was in the days of the old Pontiac Silverdome. Coach Rogers called the team over, "I was wondering if you guys could tell me how many pigeons are on the roof here."

Obviously, we had no idea. "There are 87. I counted them," said the coach, proud of his accomplishment.

I looked over at my fellow rookie, center Kevin Glover, and we didn't have to say a word. Our looks told the story, as in, *This is the NFL?*

Of course, one of the best things about being in the NFL is the money. Even an undrafted rookie gets a thrill when he cashes his first paycheck. I was no different, though, I had a lot to learn about the business of football.

**Bill Muir (Lions offense line coach)**: "One constant with Lomas was his enthusiasm. This guy was always smiling. But one day, we'd gone through our walkthrough, and I noticed that Lomas was down in the dumps. He had no smile, no bounce in his step. I pulled him aside and asked what was wrong. He told me that he had gotten his first paycheck and he thought he was going to get so much money, but he didn't even get half of that. He didn't understand what had happened. I told him to eat lunch, take a shower, and go to accounting, and they'd give him an answer. Lomas came out of the office about 90 minutes later and was on the field stretching out. He had a little more bounce in his step but was still a little gloomy.

"'What'd you find out?' I asked.

"'Taxes,' he responded."

We went 7–9 my first year but had some nice quality wins—beating the Miami Dolphins (which, of course, I loved), the Dallas Cowboys, and the New York Jets. These teams had some really good players: Hall of Famers Dan Marino, Randy White, Tony Dorsett, and the "New York Sack Exchange."

The leaders on our team were veterans like Keith Dorney, Jimmy Williams, Eric Hipple, and Leonard Thompson. Lineman Doug English was just about done as a player. My first foray into the pros was just a little off. At the time I couldn't really put a finger on it, but as I played with other teams, I realized that we had a bad team culture. Sure, we wanted to win, but there wasn't a nurturing environment. A football team needs to be like a family. Guys in our locker room were afraid to teach the younger guys who might eventually take their job. In 1985 the Lions drafted four offensive linemen, including Glover and myself. It was obvious that the team wanted to re-make the line, and the veterans knew it. There was definitely an air of distrust, which held us back as a team.

For myself, I just wanted to keep getting better, and it worked.

In early October, we played the Packers up at Lambeau Field. Green Bay's D-line ate us for lunch.

**Muir**: "The Packers had a defensive lineman named Ezra Johnson. He might have been the quickest defensive end I ever saw. Lomas was a little bit late getting started after holding out in camp."

**Bill Keenist (Lions assistant public relations director)**: "In that first game with the Packers, Ezra had a sack on Lomas, and the line had four as a group."

**Muir**: "Lomas was really struggling with Ezra, and he comes off the field and says, 'He's so quick off the ball, he's not letting me set up!' Like any good line coach, I tell Lomas, 'Cut [block] the SOB!' So the next play, Lomas cuts him. [Johnson couldn't make a play.] The next play, he cuts him again. I'm getting excited on the sideline! But the next two plays, Lomas doesn't cut him, and Ezra makes two plays.

"Lomas comes over to the sideline, and I'm right up in his face, yelling, why isn't he cut blocking him? Lomas just looks at me, and says, 'Ezra said we're not allowed to cut block a veteran.'"

**Keenist**: "What I remember is that we played [the Packers] again in the next-to-last game at the Silverdome, and Lomas just stoned him. That was sort of like, not that he needed any more validation, but to see how far he came as a rookie in just a couple of months. If there was any doubt that this guy was a Pro Bowl caliber player, that game ended it."

But the bad feelings weren't just among the players. There was a huge disconnect between us and the front office. There's always going to be a line of separation, but this was just ill will. There were several times where I know the front office instructed the coaches to make sure guys didn't hit their incentives, especially regarding playing time.

I guess that stuff might happen occasionally now, but this was blatant. Partly because of this, we hardly ever did anything in the community.

I think the media was pretty decent to us. Mike O'Hara was tough, as was Tom Kowalski. You have to remember that this was pre-Internet, so the number of reporters was fewer; there was no 24/7 coverage. Fred Hickman and Bryan Burwell were with us quite a bit, and they were fair. Legendary sportswriter Jerry Green would stop by on occasion and he was fair, too.

I'm not really sure what the fans' expectations were for the team. They had been let down so often, I don't think they really got their hopes up. As a rookie, I did a good job of not paying attention to the external pressure. It was just me going out there, trying to get better every day. I thought I was picking up the concepts pretty well.

**Rob Rubick (Lions tight end):** "He was very bright, just like James Jones—those two guys from Florida. You block a lot with the tackle as a tight end because back then we had a lot of combination blocking, a lot of communication between us, and Lom was always there. He always had the right calls on, never left you hanging. Some tackles, they may come off a double-team too quick, but Lomas would always tee them up for you, then be able to come off, and get the run through blitzers. His personality was second to none. His demeanor is refreshing. A lot of offensive linemen are gung ho, intense. Lomas was much more laid-back. He didn't play with that anger; he was more of a cerebral player.

"Lomas wasn't a leader in the sense that he'd get up and give speeches. He was a leader by his play. It didn't take very long to realize that hey, he's really good. If you're going to be a leader, it helps to be really good, and Lomas was. Very few guys would be able to come into the league and have the success he had at such a young age, but it all goes back to two things: his intelligence and his athleticism. He'd look like he was going to get beat, and that's going to happen a lot as a rookie, but he'd recover, and minimize the damage."

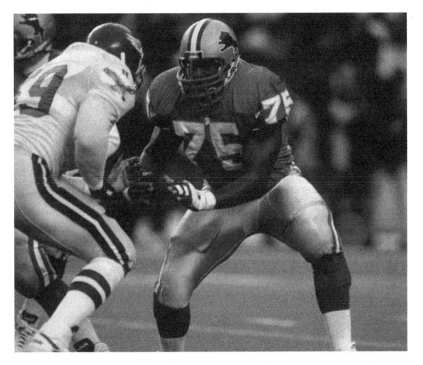

Even after playing in the SEC, the NFL represented a major transition for me. (Courtesy Detroit Lions)

After winning those seven games my first year, things got rough. The next season, our schedule was no joke. We had two matchups with the Super Bowl champion Chicago Bears and Hall of Famer

21

Richard Dent, two against the Minnesota Vikings with Hall of Famer Chris Doleman, two more with the Packers and Pro Bowler Johnson. Oh yeah, that was just in our division! We also played the Los Angeles Rams with Eric Dickerson, who only rushed for 1,821 yards. It's no wonder that we went 5–11.

We won four games each of the next two seasons. Things were clearly not heading in the right direction. One specific moment, however, put us on the right path. It was November 5, 1989, in Houston. On the surface, this was just another disappointing loss, 35–31, to the Oilers. Football is a sport where everyone needs to pull in the same direction on the field. That doesn't mean we all have to hang out together, but you need to be a team. This was the beginning of us pulling together in the locker room.

Sean Jones was a Pro Bowl defensive end for the Oilers. We knew each other and would talk during the game. During this contest Sean ran up to me and said one of my teammates had called him the n-word. Sean was livid and said he couldn't believe I would block next to a racist like him. Guys say all types of things in the heat of the moment, but I hadn't heard anyone say anything, so you just went on and played the game. Make no mistake, though, I totally believe Sean. He'd never make something like that up. The next week, our linebacker, Jimmy Williams, brought it up during a team meeting. Everyone aired their opinion, and it was over with.

Believe it or not, this was really a positive turning point for our team. From that point on, everyone got to know the guy next to us in and out of the locker room. Especially on the line, you need to know what makes the guy next to you tick, so you can count on him in the biggest spots.

\* \* \*

Before the 1989 draft, Lions general manager Chuck Schmidt asked me for the first and only time for my input about a player. I told him, of course, we had to draft Barry Sanders.

The 5'8" running back from Oklahoma State had won the Heisman Trophy, but this was before the days of every game being televised, so only a portion of the country had seen him. Detroit had a potential Hall of Fame running back in the early '80s, but Billy Sims blew out his knee, and his career was over in 1984. In the meantime, the team's stars were guys like Eric Hipple, Leonard Thompson, and James Jones.

More than anything, Barry made us relevant. Before Barry, our only national game every year was on Thanksgiving. Suddenly, we were on *Monday Night Football*. People were talking about us!

With Barry just killing everyone in the league, things were starting to come together, but the wins still were hard to find. Coach Rogers paid the price in the middle of the 1988 season and was replaced by Wayne Fontes. Talk about a cool guy, Wayne was more like a player than a coach. To be a successful player in anything, you need to have confidence, and Coach Fontes made sure we had it. He talked a big game but always believed we'd back it up.

Don't get me wrong, Coach never had trouble ripping us, but it was always behind closed doors. He used to say his big butt could take all the heat.

**Kevin Glover (Lions center)**: "He was a different cat...Wayne was one to keep it fun. We worked hard, but he wanted us to enjoy the experience and he enjoyed the experience. It was a fun era to be there. We worked hard and we had a great deal of pride in each other. Wayne trusted the players."

**Barry Sanders (Lions running back)**: "Wayne is a great guy. He didn't take himself too serious. He had played the game at a high level. He coached in the league. He was just a guy you could certainly look at as a players' coach because the players did have input into a lot of things. I think that had to do with the personality he had. Guys were pretty responsible, so I think he felt like he could treat us in a more mature way. He did not take himself too seriously. He liked to laugh. But hey, there were times when he did get serious, and I think he had a good balance of that. I think that really created a great environment. You look at where they were before Wayne took the helm, then compare it to the eight years he was here, where we had four playoff runs. That's something that his record speaks for himself. He is very likable. He liked to have a good time. He really enjoyed being an NFL coach. We all have great memories of him because he was a guy who didn't do a lot of screaming but knew how to get the best out of guys."

**Rubick**: "Wayne had been the defensive coordinator. In that role, he was very interactive, always talking, running plays with the guys all over the field. He was very positive and good in the locker room. Wayne kept it pretty simple: you play well, you win, and it goes easy. Once he became the head coach, he endeared himself with both the defense and the offense. We knew he wanted to be a head coach."

**Wayne Fontes (Lions head coach)**: "The press never wrote a bad thing about any of my players in the papers. That was one of the things I told the team. Anyone we brought in that was new, Lomas would tell them that I would never rip them publicly. I told them, 'Whatever happens behind closed doors will stay there. It's me and you'...If someone missed a block or made a bad play, you would never read about it. It was about the respect between me and the team and back to me. And I did rip them. Lomas will tell you I ripped them good sometimes, but no player I ever ripped got in my face. It was strictly us, and they liked it that way."

Playing for a guy who will take those bullets for you means everything to a player. And he'd take care of us, too. During practice, he'd make sure we weren't on our feet too much or taking too many hits. We were always a good second-half team, and I think part of the reason was that we were fresher than the other team.

If we ever needed to talk, Wayne was always welcoming.

**Glover**: "He always had an open-door policy. He had an office downstairs that had this huge sectional couch. Sometimes the leaders on the team would go down there. Guys like me, Chris Spielman, Benny Blades, Jerry Ball, and Lomas would sit on the coach, and he'd listen to us. Sometimes, he'd end up making adjustments. Other times, he's the head coach, and you had to go with what he said. But he was definitely someone you felt like you could go and talk to."

**Fontes**: "I decided I was going to have a committee of players. I wanted a couple of offensive linemen, [Lomas and Kevin Glover]. I had a linebacker with Chris Spielman. We had Jerry Ball, a nose tackle; Benny Blades, a defensive back; and, of course, Barry Sanders."

**Spielman:** "I think he's an underrated coach. Wayne realized he had pretty good leadership on that team and let the leaders lead. To me that was a sign of a good coach. He doesn't get credit for his knowledge of the game. I think what it says is that you have to recognize that the leaders will control the temperature of the practice. They won't take shortcuts. When your best players are your best leaders, you let them police themselves. It's a good combination to have. When you have it, it shows good recognition on the coach's part. I thought Wayne always had a good feeling for our team."

**Fontes:** "Lomas was in charge of the committee, and I wanted to be able to relate to my players. I wanted my players to know that I was going to treat them like men, like I wanted to be treated, and Lomas understood that...we'd have practice on a hot day, and Lomas would come in and he'd say, 'Coach, the committee's been talking...And he'd be sitting on my couch with that big body of his and he'd look me dead in the eyes, and say, 'The fellas think we need a day with our pads off today.' I asked, 'What fellas?' He just said, 'The team. Our legs have been getting kind of heavy.' So I said okay. We'd practice without pads.

"I trusted Lomas, I trusted his instincts about the players and how everybody was feeling during two-a-days, and he left my office. All of the players would be sitting in the locker room, waiting to put their pads on, not knowing what Lomas was going to say coming out of the office. And I heard Lomas, say, 'No pads!' And the guys would go crazy, and start chanting, 'Lo-Mas, Lo-Mas, Lo-Mas!'"

Our special teams coach was a guy by the name of Frank Gansz. He was the perfect guy for that job because this dude was

26

I-N-T-E-N-S-E. But he loved us. Coach had a great saying: "I'm not attacking the person; I'm attacking the problem. The problem is anything that will prevent us from achieving at the highest level."

That was part of our pieces coming together. We had the best running back in football, coaches that we'd run through a wall for, and after the n-word incident, we were paying closer attention to being better teammates.

If we felt like Wayne was taking too many bullets for us, our team leaders—guys like Bennie Blades, Spielman, Glover, William White, Jerry Ball, and myself—would call a meeting, and we'd all be 100 percent up front. One guy might tell another he didn't like him, and we'd move on. What happened in the locker room stayed there. There was no pillow talk, where a guy would come home to his wife, and tell her what was going on. It was just between us.

We were a confident team; we took the field *knowing* we were going to beat the other team. We knew how good we could be, and a lot of that was due to the environment that Coach Fontes fostered. That's why we knew when he was in trouble that we needed to step it up. We had a good thing and didn't want to lose it. We were one helluva team and part of that comes from our coach.

# Chapter 3

# Some Players Fit Like a Glove, Some Don't

Once my college career came to a close, I was selected to play in a few All-Star Games. One of those, the 1985 Senior Bowl, gave me one of the best friends in my life.

Kevin Glover was a quiet kid from Washington, D.C., who played center for a pretty good University of Maryland team. The Terps had won a couple of ACC titles in a row, but they were not on the national level like Florida, FSU, or Miami. We definitely hit it off from the get-go.

**Kevin Glover (Lions center)**: "It was a different era then. It wasn't the era of the Internet, knowing where all the players are, where the linemen in the country were ranked. When I was invited to the Senior Bowl, I kind of went through the roster to see which players were playing in different bowl games. I knew that Lomas had made first-team All-America as one of the best linemen in the country but didn't know him personally.

"I got to the hotel, and Lo had checked in before I did, then went out for a while. I got into the room, and there was a shirt there with extremely long sleeves. His helmet was there along with his shoes. I said this guy must be humungous! He walked into the room with a huge smile, and that's how we initially met.

"It was the natural bond of being offensive linemen, both having a great deal of pride in our programs...we both had a lot of pride in the teammates we had played with in the past. He played with James Jones, who was a previous first-round pick with the Lions, and I played with Boomer Esiason and Ron Solt, who had been a first-round pick the previous year. A lot of our early conversations were about the pride in the organizations we played in, the great players we played with, and great coaches we played for.

"I think one of the things that gave us a bond kind of early on is that we would stay and do extra running after practice even at the Senior Bowl, so we both had this type of commitment to stay in top shape and work extra even if other people weren't willing to."

Once the Senior Bowl was over, we figured we'd play against each other in the pros. But then a funny thing happened. My day was over quickly, as the Lions took me at No. 6. Glove was in for a surprise.

**Glover:** "I actually had a paper due that morning, so I worked on it late the night before...I had heard the stories and seen some of the issues with guys not getting drafted as highly as they had thought, so I didn't want to sit there waiting and went over to my parents' house and took a nap.

"Strangely, the Patriots, who were doing well and were one of the top teams in the league, called. They had the last pick in the first round. [They originally owned the 16th pick but traded with the San Francisco 49ers, who drafted legendary wide receiver Jerry Rice.] New England told me that if I was still there for their selection they were going to draft me. When it came to their turn, they chose Trevor Matich from BYU [who eventually came to the Lions as a backup]. Back then, I had no idea if I was going in the first, second, or any round. I just wanted the opportunity to play. The Lions called me, and I was picked by them six picks later."

How sweet was that? I make a new, close friend, and now we're playing on the same team! Kev was a lot more low-key than me, but for whatever reason, we mixed. He came along with the Lions a little more slowly than me. I started from Day One. He battled with injuries and didn't crack the lineup until his second year. I like to say we brought the craziness out of each other.

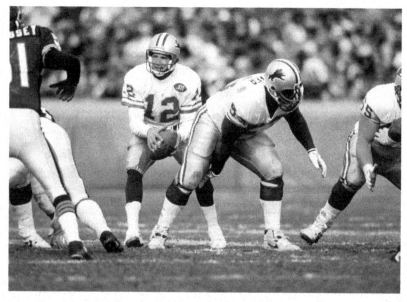

Snapping the ball to Erik Kramer against the Bears, center Kevin Glover and I became very close on and off the field.

Glove and I played alongside each other for 11 years. We experienced some really, really highs...and some really, really lows. My first few years when I felt like I was getting a raw deal in not getting picked for the Pro Bowl, Glove was a great sounding board. Truth is, he should have made more Pro Bowls himself—he made three—but when your team doesn't win, you don't get to go. That's one of the reasons we'd get on Scott Mitchell. He was getting paid regardless. For an offensive lineman, we need to win games and we didn't feel like Scott was fully committed.

Glove and I lived together for our first couple of years in Rochester, Michigan. It was there where I first learned about the thrills of snow. Coming from Florida, I had never seen snow, and it was awesome. I even went out and did some snow angels.

**Glover**: "He came running into my room at 4:30 AM and almost knocked the door off the hinges. He's yelling, 'Glove, Glove, it's snowing! Come look out the front window!' I'm like Lomas, if it's snowing out the front window, then it's snowing out the back window, too. Now get out of my room! It's 4:30 in the morning!'"

**Wayne Fontes (Lions head coach)**: "He was cold *all* the time. When the first snow hit, Lomas had more clothes on than Santa Claus. I said, 'What's going on, big fella?' And he said, 'Coach, it's cooooooold!'"

The next year, we stayed in the house of our former teammate, Larry Lee, after he was traded to the Miami Dolphins. Being a part of a losing team was not easy. A lot of weeks, we'd stay in and fall asleep watching *Monday Night Football*. When you're team stinks, I don't think it's right to be out at the clubs.

As we grew into veterans, we took on more leadership. We always made sure that no other linemen would beat us in sprints. We went to Coach Fontes and asked if we could train some of the younger guys, and it worked out well. We helped to create a different environment than we had walked into. If you do a good enough job of teaching the younger players, it carries on even after you leave.

Glove was a guy I could bounce things off of. He went through all the battles with me, so we knew exactly what each of us was dealing with. On the field I knew if I was getting beat, he'd have my back and call out a different line formation. I don't know where I'd be without him.

\* \* \*

Now we had our coach, line, and running back settled. So at the 1990 NFL Draft, the Lions decided to get us a franchise quarterback. Rodney Peete had started for half the year, but he was a sixth-round pick and unproven. He had shown some promise, but he still threw more interceptions (nine) than touchdowns (five).

We had the seventh pick that year, and it was like the draft fell perfectly for us. For whatever reason, there were more high-pick flops than most years. Jeff George went first to the Indianapolis Colts, and that was followed by Blair Thomas going to the New York Jets. (Other first-round busts included Keith McCants with the Tampa Bay Buccaneers and Chris Singleton with the Patriots.) In the first six picks, there were two future Hall of Famers. The Seattle Seahawks picked Cortez Kennedy, while the San Diego Chargers selected Junior Seau. The Chicago Bears also drafted Pro Bowl safety Mark Carrier. Our quarterback of the future was sitting for us at No. 7.

Andre Ware had won the Heisman, throwing 46 touchdowns for the University of Houston. The Cougars played the run-and-shoot offense, which placed a premium on throwing but not on protecting the quarterback. Our offensive coordinator, Mouse Davis, was the founder of the run-and-shoot. This was a perfect marriage.

Or at least it should have been.

There's always a debate about whether rookie quarterbacks should play right away or sit and learn on the bench. I think you get better by playing in games. Since Andre was already familiar with our offense, he should have been our quarterback. Instead, the coaches decided not to rush him, so Rodney began the season under center and started the first eight games.

Andre finally got his chance in Week 9 against the Minnesota Vikings—sort of. He was so bad (5-of-11, two interceptions) that he got benched, and Bob Gagliano, a former 12th- round pick, replaced him. Dre's confidence was shot.

I know what Wayne and Mouse were trying to do by bringing him along slowly. The run-and-shoot leaves five guys blocking seven defenders—not a good ratio—but this guy mastered the offense in college and would have been fine playing right away. And it's not like he didn't have the tools. I saw him throw a 70-yard bomb off the wrong foot. Andre started only six games during his four-year NFL career, throwing just five touchdowns. A whole career undermined by a bad start.

# Chapter 4

# The Inspiration of Mike Utley

Nobody ever asks me who the best player I ever teamed up with was. The answer is obvious—Barry. But the most inspirational teammate I had was hands down (but thumb up), Mike Utley.

Offensive linemen toil in obscurity. Most of the time when you hear one of our names being called, it's because we either got a penalty or screwed up, and the quarterback gets sacked. Don't feel sorry for us. We love protecting our guys. But most of the time, nobody knows who we are. John Madden was really the first announcer to talk positively about us.

Because of that anonymity, linemen are close, really close. For us to have any success, we have to be. A running back or defensive end can be out of position, and a teammate can cover for them. Not us. A good offensive line needs to work like a hand in a glove. If one of us screws up, nine times out of 10, the play won't work. We're playing in a hostile situation with 80,000 fans screaming on the road, and our quarterback calls an audible. I can't hear him from my tackle position, but the guard next to me can. I've got to have total trust that he can relay the play to me. On a combination block, I need to do my part without worrying about the guy next to me because I know he's going to do his.

My linemates and me are brothers. We lift together, we party together, we take the same bus to the game. Race doesn't matter. We're all equal and we spend more time together than we do with our own families.

Mike Utley was different than the rest of us. He was a hippie—straight out of Washington State University when he came to Detroit in 1989, and we gave him a lot of crap. He was all grunge and had a mullet (that he still has to this day) and he was physically weak. When he first came to town, this 6'6" dude couldn't even bench 200 pounds! But he was our kid brother. We used to call him Beetlejuice, because of his small head like the guy in the movie. But Mike made himself into one of us. He worked as hard as anyone and he got what we were trying to do.

**Kevin Glover (Lions center)**: "Mike had a wide body, big shoulders, a little head, so we teased him about that. Everybody has a nickname, especially the rookies. They get labeled with certain names, and it sticks with them for the rest of their life. It's really a way of saying we really like you, you're going to be good, and we want you to be a part of our unit. And he definitely did that immediately.

"Mike wasn't the strongest guy on the line when he got there upper-body wise, but he was really powerful in the lower body. For an offensive lineman, it's about leverage, quickness, and he had all the tools to be good. He was really smart. One great thing for Mike was that he wasn't a young guy who would shy away from advice from the older guys. He was a very coachable guy, he loved spending time with us, and he was a little bit of a rebel, too. I remember one time asking him, 'Did I really see you out there, pulling a wheelie on this motorcycle?' He was like, 'Yeah, that was me.' He had this really nice motorcycle, went really fast. Here was this guy who was 6'6," riding a sport bike with his mullet hairdo flying in the wind. So he was a bit of a different breed, but we actually loved that about him."

**Mike Utley (Lions offensive lineman)**: "I was the only rookie there at that time. Coming from being a consensus All-American from Washington State, a four-year starter, to all of a sudden, showing up at a facility where everybody knows everybody.

"At least people had been there during spring ball, so they're comfortable. They've been in the league for at least one year, the majority more...All of a sudden, you come in, and no one likes you, no one wants you, no one cares about you. That's the No. 1 thing. No. 2 is you have a long hair, bleached hair, earring-wearing kind of a guy coming in, and if you do ask a question of Lomas or Glove or whoever, you're lucky to get an answer because they don't want you there.

"I understand that, but that was business. The gameplan as you're there is that you have to prove yourself on every occasion tremendously. You earn your right to be one of the men. At that point, I wasn't one of the men. Lomas was. Glove was. Eric Andolsek was. They were all there. You had to prove yourself. I was doing everything I could to first believe in myself, secondly, to do what I always did in college; do the little things other people aren't willing to do...and that's what I tried to do.

"Let's put it this way. When they're barking at you and yelling at you, they're there. When they stop yelling, you're done; you're no longer relevant at that point in time. And that is absolutely right. What they did was treat me like a rookie scum, which is the way you should be treated, but they wanted to see if I could hold up to what it takes to be a professional.

"When guys are jabbing you, they're seeing if you can earn the right to be one of them. That's the ticket, but I knew that. Just keep your nose clean, learn your plays, do the things people don't want to do, show up early, stay late. And if you're talented, you will make it. If you're not, you'll just go by the wayside. I earned the right to be one of them. I wasn't there yet, but I had the right to be one of them."

He definitely did. On and off the field, we all loved that guy before November 17, 1991, but since that day, we've loved him even more.

We were playing the Rams in Los Angeles, and I was on the sideline with a separated shoulder from the week before. We were down 10–7 at the end of the third quarter. On the very first play of the fourth, Rams lineman David Rocker jumped in the air to try and bat down a pass. (He failed, as Erik Kramer hit and connected with Robert Clark on an 11-yard touchdown.) Mike pushed forward and fell. Rocker fell on him.

The result was devastating. Mike had fractured the sixth and seventh vertebrae in his neck. Now remember, guys go down on seemingly every play in the NFL, but it was pretty clear right away that this was something major.

My first inclination that Mike was in trouble was when Glove came off the field with tears in his eyes.

**Glover**: "It was a normal play, a deep crossing route, which we threw for a touchdown...We had a tradition that when you scored a TD, you achieved your goal, so we'd run down in the end zone to celebrate. I remember turning around looking for Mike Utley because normally I'd tease him to stop jumping on my back because he'd be so excited to celebrate. If you weren't paying attention, he'd turn around and get you. I turned around and saw that he was lying down, so I went to him and asked if he was okay. Just the look in his eyes, you knew something about it wasn't a normal injury. Mike was tough as they come. He was never one to stay down if he wasn't seriously injured. Just the look in his eyes was pretty frightening. Then as the doctors and trainers started to evaluate him...you'd see them pulling down his socks and pinching his legs, pinching his upper legs, his stomach, pulling up his shirt, trying to find the area where he had feeling, you just knew it was something tragic."

**Barry Sanders (Lions running back):** "It almost felt like someone had died. It was that serious. I think it just shook everyone up."

The thing about Mike is that his spirit is incredible. As he was laying on the stretcher being carried off, he was paralyzed, but Mike was thinking about everyone else. That's the only way I can figure out how he willed himself to give the fans a thumbs up sign. Everyone always will remember that. As an athlete you can't take the field worrying about injury. That's the best way to get yourself hurt. It never enters your mind. I felt guilty that I wasn't on the field next to Mike that day. Maybe that play would have developed differently, who knows?

One thing I know is that I *never* could have handled things the way Mike did. I would have just shut down, not letting anyone see me. But not Mike. I can honestly say that I've never seen him feeling down. Even now, all these years later, when we speak, he tells me that he's going to walk.

**Sanders:** "Mike has handled it so well. He has been a great encouragement. That made it a lot easier for us being able to cope with it. It was a tremendous impact on all of us young men at that time and even to today. You realize how serious the game was and is."

Lions trainers attend to Mike Utley after the offensive lineman suffers a horrific neck injury. (AP Images)

Seeing him go down was like watching a relative become paralyzed. All the fans saw the thumbs up, but they didn't see him in the hospital like we did, fighting, never giving up. I can only imagine the pain he was in, being a 300-pound world-class athlete, being unable to move his legs. We all wanted to do everything for him. We were on a mission to show him how much we care about him, and it was draining on us. Draining, but so inspirational. Mike is a no-nonsense guy, who has never felt sorry for himself. He's never changed a bit.

**Bill Keenist (Lions assistant public relations director)**: "Injuries are hard to deal with...season-ending are hard to deal with, but Mike's was a life changer. It was nothing that any of us had ever had to deal with, let alone the guys on the field. You're lining up next to a guy who's fighting for his life."

**Utley**: "If you allow someone to make you afraid, then it's your fault. If you allow someone to make you addicted to something, it's your fault. Be responsible. I chose to play this game, the Ford family gave me the opportunity to play this game, I got to play with some great athletes. I wasn't going to let them down, the Ford family down, or myself down, and allow this to affect me in a negative way. That is a choice, and that is how I've always believed it."

Knowing Mike, that's him in a nutshell. Here's a guy who can't walk, but he drives, goes skydiving, does all the stuff he wants to do. We know what we sign up for playing in the NFL, and Mike has never been bitter.

**Utley**: "Just the other day, we were on the phone busting chops back and forth. It's just what we do! If I didn't have respect for Big Daddy, if he didn't have respect for me, none of this would have happened. In the meeting rooms, the way we busted chops on each other, a weaker person would have walked away in tears. That's just the way it is with us...Over the years Lomas has become a friend, and he knows what that means to me."

It doesn't surprise me that this giant of a man took the fight of his life and is running a foundation that helps people with special abilities. He was always thinking of others. I pray that he does walk someday.

Although we were emotionally spent by Mike's accident in 1991, his positive energy inspired us the rest of the season. After that win against Los Angeles, we were 7–4. We won out from there.

Mike's "thumbs up" was the perfect rallying point. We created T-shirts and we talked about it every day. There was no question that everything was dedicated to our brother.

**Keenist**: "Mike gets hurt, then we go to Minnesota, and Barry has 220 yards, four touchdowns—just a remarkable performance."

**Sanders**: "I don't know what happened. It just seemed like the guys couldn't touch me. It's really hard to explain. I had other good days, but that particular game—and they had a pretty good defense at that time—I don't want to say mysterious, but it just seemed strange. They couldn't lay a hand on me, and when they did get close, it was like they just fell off. I just don't know what happened that week."

I just remember how crazy Sanders had Joey Browner, the Pro Bowl safety of the Vikings, looking that game. Barry just exploded. I mean Joey was the real deal, but Barry was on a tear, and nobody could stop him. I remember Henry Thomas (who was on the Vikings and later played with us) telling the story of how they'd get ready for

Barry. Talk about old school, the coaches would bring a chicken on the field, and the defense would try and run it down.

That might have made for a good dinner, but it didn't matter. He was like a magician in cleats. I think one of the underrated advantages for Barry was that he was so small that he could hang behind us and then burst out of nowhere. He'd be gone with that explosion. Against the Vikings that day, our blocking scheme was solid. Our biggest job was to get Barry to the second level of the defense. Once we got him through the first level, then he could do his magic. A lot of teams figured that out. That's why they'd try to get through the first level and tackle him for a loss. Because once he got to the second level, it was hard to contain him. We got him to the second level a lot during that game.

Although a lot was made of No. 20's improvisational skills, I'd always think back to practice, and it would seem like déjà vu. The same stuff we'd see in games, we'd have already experienced in practice. Whenever I played with other running backs, I'd tell them to emulate Barry and run the play all the way to the end. Barry would do that, so when the game came, he already knew if he was going to shake this guy left or right or stiff-arm his guy because he had worked on it over and over. On almost every play, Barry would run all the way to the end zone. I still remember Bennie Blades trying to chase him down. When the games came, it all slowed down for Barry.

\* \* \*

Eleven days after the Utley injury, we hosted Chicago in the Thanksgiving Day game. There was no chance the Bears were coming into our house—the first home game since Mike's injury—and beating us. We had such a quiet confidence. It was obvious we were going to do something. We were riding high off that adrenaline. I credit a lot of that to Mike.

We went to see Mike after his injury. But first we huddled up and talked about what we were going to say and not say in the room, because we didn't want Mike to feel a certain way. When we left out of that room, Mike had us jacked up like we could do anything. He wouldn't let us feel sorry for ourselves. It was easy to carry on business that next week. Plus, you're kind of carrying that chip on your shoulder, like, *Hey, our teammate is down, our teammate gave us the thumbs up and really encouraged us to go out and fight the rest of the season for him.*

Barry says that Minnesota game was easy, but really, the rest of that season was that way for us. After that happened we were on such an emotional high that we didn't lose another game the rest of that season. Mike made it easy for us not to turn the page but also not to wallow in sorrow for what happened to him. He encouraged us that he was going to fight this injury, and we continued to fight that season for him. I remember us being so confident. When we went out onto the field, we knew we were going to win the game. We just didn't know how. That's how confident we were, and it showed in the way we played. And it all started on Thanksgiving against the Bears.

That game provided one of the highlights of my life—in or out of football. The team had come to me as a captain and asked me to give the pregame speech to the team and the crowd.

**Keenist**: "We're coming back to play the Bears on Thanksgiving on national TV—a critically important game, and we're still dealing with Mike's reality. On the plane home, it sort of hit me that we might have an opportunity to do what we ended up doing. I ended up writing the words on a piece of paper. It just started coming to me, so I wrote the words out. 'Hey Mike, we know you're listening, we want you to know you're as big a part of this team as you ever were.' That type of thing. So I went to my boss and said, 'Why don't you let me run with this? I think I can get the networks to run with this and carry it live. I think it will be profoundly impactful and appropriate. First and foremost, it will be so important for Mike to hear this, it will be so important for the team to know they're talking to Mike.'"

Of course, it was a huge honor, being asked to deliver this pregame speech, but I originally declined. It wasn't that I didn't want to help, but when you're getting ready to play in an NFL game, you need to get in the zone. I knew anything with Mike would make me emotional and didn't want to take away from my concentration. Eventually, I changed my mind and I'm so glad I did. Giving that speech, letting Mike know we missed him, and giving the thumbs up was one of the best things I've ever done in my life. It provided the bond that Mike and I still have even today.

**Keenist**: "There was no one I wanted to do it more than Lomas. He was absolutely the guy...you talk about reality TV, and there was nothing more impactful than what Lomas did that day. The impact it had on our team, Lomas, and on Mike, most importantly...and quite frankly, I thought it would energize the crowd. We won the coin toss, and Mel Gray took it 45 yards to set up the first score of the game...it was something that none of us will ever forget."

**Utley**: "That Thanksgiving day, they put a TV in my room. That was 12 days after my injury. I had my brother and a buddy come in. We had some pizza, and a couple of cold ones, and they wanted to make sure I had access to a TV. I saw Lomas and the guys, right then and there, I thought it was the coolest thing in the whole wide world. That's how much emotion I got. That was big time, it really was big time. To sit there and do anything else but say how cool it was would disregard everyone's effort to make sure they're pulling for me No. 1, but also pushing me even more than that. That's how I looked at it, more the pushing than the pulling for. People push you to win. The ones that care about you—the mothers and fathers, brothers and sisters, close friends, they push you. Yes, there's emotion, but they push you to be your best. I'm not going to let anyone down without giving my 100 percent best."

**Chris Spielman (Lions linebacker)**: "Mike set the standard for us. It was our job to honor Mike the way we could—to play and to play well. When you play for an extra purpose, a righteous one—and playing for Mike was a righteous one—it's a powerful combination."

The game itself wasn't great to watch, as we scored one touchdown and three Eddie Murray field goals, but we did win it for Mike 16–6.

Even before the injury, Coach Fontes never had to worry about getting on us. We had leaders like Jerry Ball, Bennie Blades, Chris Spielman, and myself. There was an unspoken bond. We could step on each other's toes to get our point across. I remember times when Spielman would come right up to me and say, "Lomas, you need to do a better job, or we're not going to win." Like Coach Gansz said, "we're attacking the problem, not the person." One thing you see with a lot of successful teams is that they self-police. That's what we had.

* * *

We ended up winning the NFC Central division title (the team's first since 1957) and hosted the big, bad Dallas Cowboys in the play-offs. This team had future Hall of Famers Troy Aikman, Emmitt Smith, and Michael Irvin. In the next four years, these guys would win three Super Bowls.

But not in our house.

We had the perfect storm. Our crowd was the loudest I've ever played in front of. We matched them man for man and just physically dominated them. Erik Kramer never got touched and had a huge game. We used lots of short throws, and he got the ball out of his hands quickly. Barry didn't have his best statistical game, but he was magnificent. Our receivers played a great game. The Silverdome was so loud that we couldn't even hear our teammates talk on the sideline. The final was 38–6, and Wayne got a Gatorade bath as time wound down. We were on cloud nine.

That meant that this season not only represented our first division championship since 1957, but it was also the last time Detroit had won a playoff game. Next thing we knew, it was the NFC Championship Game in Washington. This would be no easy task. In the season opener, the Redskins crushed us 45–0. The Skins had a pretty good quarterback in Mark Rypien, who was in the midst of a career year, with receivers like the great Art Monk and Ricky Sanders. They had a good defense with All-Pro Charles Mann and my boy from Florida, Wilber Marshall. And all of that added up to a 14–2 season. We felt disrespected, and Las Vegas listed Washington as a 14-point favorite. RFK Stadium was a tough place to play. The field would actually vibrate from the stands. Of course, they still had "the Hogs," who were seeking their third championship in 10 years. (They had also lost one.)

But we were pretty confident. I thought we had already beaten the more dangerous team in Dallas. Looking back at it, it might have been one coaching decision that got us off on the wrong foot. The way we lined up, Fred Stokes was over me, and Mann took on our rookie, Scott Conover. That was a mismatch. What we *should* have done was slide the protection to help Scott. I had Stokes taken care of, no problem. For whatever reason we did the opposite. And we paid quickly.

On the second play of the game, Mann blew past Conover, stripped Kramer of the ball, and the Redskins were in business. Two plays later, Gerald Riggs took it in for the score, and we were down 7–0. We never recovered. They throttled us 41–10, and that was that.

In retrospect, I don't think we ever got into the right frame of mind. The city understood how big a deal this opportunity was, but the players probably didn't. I was devastated after this one, but had no idea the worse pain was yet to come.

### More Tragedy on Top of Defeat

Once the season ended, we started to realize what a successful season we had—12–4, the division crown, and doing it all for our teammate, who was fighting for his life.

I lived not too far from the Silverdome, and as everyone was packing up, a bunch of the guys stopped by my house, to hang out.

One of those guys was Eric Andolsek, who was making a stop before driving home to Louisiana.

We called the offensive line "The Fantastic Four." Eric was built like a table. He was the live version of Barney Rubble—squat and strong. "Rock" was coming into his own, starting 48 straight games since the end of his rookie season.

That June someone from the Lions called me and delivered the news: Eric had been killed in a truck accident at his house. This was impossible. First, this guy was 25 years old! Second, there's no way something like this could happen less than a year after Mike's injury.

**Glover**: "It was such a freaky thing. It was the offseason. At the time Eric, Lomas, and I all had the same agent, Mark Bartelstein out of Chicago. My wife and I just happened to be on vacation. It wasn't the cell phone era. We had cell phones, but you didn't have it with you all the time. I just happened to call into my agent one day to see how negotiations were going for myself and Eric, and the secretary was crying and passed the phone, and I was like, 'What's going on? What's wrong with her?' He knew that I had no idea what had happened, that Eric had passed away, and that's how I found out. We left from vacation, drove home, and flew down to Louisiana immediately, just a gathering for teammates and family."

The circumstances are still hard to believe. Eric told his wife, Cheryl, that he was going to be out late fishing, but that he'd weed the front yard before leaving. As fate would have it, their house was just up against a state road. She and their children were returning home. Seconds later, a truck driver, found to have cocaine in his system, plows into him going 50 mph, without even hitting the brakes.

We got word of his death and that they weren't going to be holding his body for long, so a bunch of us flew to New Orleans, and drove out to Thibodeaux, where his family lived.

This was classic small-town country. We pulled up on a state road, just one lane. We went in and tried to comfort Cheryl, but she was in so much pain. I mean, nobody expects to lose his or her spouse at 25 years old. We walked out to the front yard, and we could see his blood on the grass from where he was hit. This guy was so strong that he got hit by the truck, got thrown about 150 feet, and still lived until he got to the hospital. Unreal.

On the field, we never recovered from Eric's death. We were one of the best lines in the NFL and suddenly we had one guy paralyzed and another run over by a truck. This wasn't like a guy blowing out his knee. This was just devastating. Really, the only positive thing I can remember is that we did stay together as a team.

**Wayne Fontes (Lions head coach)**: "That was such a difficult time. I also lost my brother that year—then the whole deal with Utley and Andolsek—if you didn't have a leader in the locker room, that ship would have crumbled. I was very fortunate to have guys, especially Lomas, that held things together. It was kind of like a battle cry: 'This is us. Let's live through these guys who are less fortunate.' I was very blessed to have Lomas to hold things together."

The best thing anyone can say about that next season, in 1992, is that it was over. We had made such an emotional run to the NFC Championship Game after Mike's injury, that we were spent. With Eric's death, that put us down two offensive linemen. From a football standpoint, that's tough to overcome.

Mike had just been coming into his own when he got hurt. He had the size and he was mean. He had good techniques. That was going to be tough to replace. Eric was on the verge of becoming a Pro Bowler. This guy was really good. I knew that he was going to end up replacing me as the best offensive lineman on the team.

After spending so much time developing into one cohesive unit, we now were forced to replace 40 percent of the line. As I've said, you have to work together, hand in a glove. That was too much for us to overcome that season. That was the personnel aspect of it. Of course, we were also dealing with the personal standpoint. I mean to have one guy paralyzed, and the other killed in his early 20s and with young kids, it's like something you'd see in the movies or read about in the paper. You just have to wonder what the hell was going on.

The Lions did try to help us by hiring a team psychiatrist. Unfortunately, the sad fact is that there was so much mistrust between management and the players that it could never work.

Hardly anyone went to the counselor because we feared that whatever we said might go back to ownership. Plus, we're big, strong football players. We're not supposed to be weak, but that's the stigma, however wrong that may be, that you'd have if you went for help.

The NFL, and professional sports in general, really doesn't give you a chance to grieve. I guess part of it is because situations like Mike and Eric don't happen too often. But we finished the playoffs in January and then two months later we were back in, lifting weights, getting back to our routine. As a rule, I don't know if that's good or bad because it does help take your mind off what's going on, but it doesn't really give you a chance to wrap your head around what's happened.

That year we went 5–11, and to some, it looked like an emotional hangover from the previous season.

**Spielman:** "I don't look at it that way. We didn't respond well. We were 5–11. We just weren't good enough. The tragic things that happen, life goes on, man. Our careers don't stop. If anyone used that as an excuse—we weren't good enough."

The fact is that the games go on, and in the NFL, it's about winning. Wayne made a point of saying that to us. Winning is the only thing. Point blank. But in this game, you can't look for the easy answer. No excuses.

People, especially in sports, talk about how things like this put life into perspective, and for me, it was really true. Mike's injury and Eric's death changed the way I looked at life forever.

Back in 1987 we drafted a guy named Reggie Rogers, out of the University of Washington. Reggie was a crazy athlete, the seventh pick overall. He even played college basketball. His brother, Don, was an All-American at UCLA, a first-round pick by the Cleveland Browns. But he overdosed on drugs and died at 23 years old.

Unfortunately, Reggie never learned from his brother. I really liked Reggie. I'm even the godfather of his daughter. Reggie had a substance problem in college, and the Lions wanted some of us older guys to look over him. As it turned out, nothing would save Reggie from himself. During his rookie year, Reggie only played six games due to what the team called emotional problems. We knew he was getting into drugs. Some of us went to crackhouses in Pontiac, Michigan, trying to rescue him.

Five games into his second season, Reggie hit another car and killed three teenagers. As it turned out, he had a blood alcohol level one-and-a-half times the legal limit.

Reggie broke his neck in the crash, and his time in Detroit was over. He went to prison, then came back to play one year with the Buffalo Bills and one with the Tampa Bay Buccaneers. He died in 2013—high on cocaine. It's amazing how much can happen to one group of guys.

**Glover**: "I have a pic in the weight room of my house of the wives from that year. My wife always talks about how close the wives were on our team, not just the players. To look at that photo— Stephanie Spielman is no longer with us. [She died from breast cancer.] She was a huge part of the wives' connection. Cheryl Andolsek was in the picture; Eric is no longer with us. Toby Caston and his wife are in the photo, and he's no longer with us [car accident]. There was a lot that happened in that span with pieces of your family disappearing, so it was a tough era for us. Lomas and I, being the oldest guys on the team—or definitely the oldest on the offensive line at the time—it was a big part of our responsibility to keep everyone heading in the right direction, staying together."

Chapter 5

# Mr. Football: Chris Spielman

In 1988 the Lions drafted one of those guys who would become the heartbeat of the franchise. If there was ever a guy meant to play football, it had to be Chris Spielman. I mean the guy was born in Canton, Ohio, the home of the Pro Football Hall of Fame! And there's no doubt in my mind that had he not been derailed by injuries, he'd have a bust at the Hall.

This guy was *all* football. He ate, slept, and breathed it. He was 100 percent totally consumed by it. Now, I may be old, but I never played with Green Bay Packers great Ray Nitschke. But he and Chris were the same player. This is a guy who, as he was growing up, would put hot dogs in his pants and socks, so that the dogs in the neighborhood would chase him around. He did all of this just so he could improve his footwork.

Chris was a guy who never sought the spotlight. He was the first high school football player ever to be on the box of Wheaties, but it was only because his coaches did it without consulting him. One year he called his coach to open the gym so that he could lift weights... on Christmas. When Chris was five years old, his grandmother came over. Little Chris sprinted toward her and tackled her. But as Chris likes to say: "Like a true Spielman, she got right up." She broke her arm, but a legend was born.

When Chris was in high school, he was considering attending the University of Michigan. His father told him that was fine, but that he'd never be allowed in his parents' house again. Chris ended up at Ohio State. Getting drafted by the Cleveland Browns would have been the fairytale story, but I'm sure glad he ended up in Detroit. It was a perfect match. Chris was a total Midwest guy, a blue-collar guy who played hard. He went above and beyond what was expected. And he played hurt.

I remember one season Spielman tore his pectoral muscle. That's an injury that usually ends your season. Not for this guy. His chest was all black and blue, and he had to put on a brace just to be able to raise his arm, but that's what we needed, so that's what he did. He'd put himself in harm's way if it would help the team.

When you play in the NFL for 18 years, you come across some interesting dudes. Chicago Bears linebacker Mike Singletary was the most intense guy I ever played against. John Randle, Lawrence Taylor, both Hall of Famers, were both off the charts with their drive and desire. Chris belongs in that group. But you can't talk about Chris without talking about Stephanie.

Chris and Stephanie were college sweethearts, and she was his alter ego. That crazy, super-intense guy on the field? When he was around Stephanie—and eventually their four children—it was a 180-degree change. They say opposites attract, and that was true about those two. She was such a calming influence. As intense as he was, she was the opposite.

Being the wife of a professional athlete isn't easy. People talk about how great Chris was at his job, and he was, but Steph was even better at hers—being a mother. You've heard the saying, "happy wife, happy life"? I think that's true in every business but especially in sports, where we're judged on a daily basis. When things at home are good, you feel like you can tackle anything. Your mind is clear, and it's easy to focus on the job. When you've got issues at home, it's easy to carry them on to the field.

Stephanie was just awesome. Just like her husband, she took a strong leadership role, organizing different activities like fashion shows and fund-raisers. She just had a way to get through to her husband. We'd have Christmas parties, and it was really eye-opening to see him in that light. One year, I think he even dressed up as Santa Claus.

Chris Spielman was a very tough, very old-school linebacker who made the ulti-mate sacrifice when his wife became ill.

Stephanie was determined, too. She had such a long battle with breast cancer, fighting it four times before passing away at 42 years old. After fighting off a neck injury while playing for the Buffalo Bills, Chris took the 1998 season off to care for Stephanie and their children. People asked me if I was surprised since football players are dealing with such a short window anyway. I mean, missing a whole season is a huge deal. But it didn't surprise me in the least. She was his soulmate; he'd lay down his life for her. As much as Chris loved football, he loved Stephanie and his kids a whole lot more.

I was with Chris with the Cleveland Browns when he tried to come back after neck surgery and the year off, when he was caring for his family. It was tough to see a guy who was such a warrior who was now unable to perform the way he wanted to. Mentally, he was still that hungry 25-year-old, ready to do whatever it took. If you play in the NFL long enough, 95 percent of all players go out that way. We're just not able to physically cut it anymore. It didn't make it any easier to see though.

Chris has always been very complimentary of me. To hear Chris say such nice things about me means *everything*. Off the field we were totally different. He was all football, and I had other interests, but that's the beauty of sports. You've got all different types of people from different backgrounds all coming together for a common cause. There's nothing more important than respect from your teammates. That's why a no-nonsense guy like Chris giving me some props means so much. This is a guy who was born to play middle linebacker, and not many did it better.

It was a different time when we played together for the Lions. After the games guys wouldn't go their own way; we'd all go out together. There were Thursday dinners, family events. Players now don't do that as much, and they're really missing out. These relationships last a lot longer than our actual playing careers. I'm proud to have played with Chris and even prouder to call him a friend.

I get asked all the time if I'm surprised that such a crazy, intense guy like Chris is doing so well at his new career, calling football games for ESPN. I say yes *and* no. His personality is definitely not what you'd expect. Chris could have made a ton of money during his career with endorsements and commercials, but that wasn't him. The fact that he's been so successful at TV? No, that's not a surprise in the least. The way he prepared for games, the studying he did, I knew it would translate and I'm glad he's doing so well.

# Chapter 6
# Building an Offense

When people think about the Lions offense, obviously, the name that comes to mind is Barry Sanders. The guy is arguably the best running back in the history of the game. But our offensive line was pretty good, too. One group that gets overlooked is our receivers. Over a seven-year span, the team really did a great job of putting together a special group.

The biggest name, of course, was Herman Moore, out of the University of Virginia. He came in 1991, as we were trying to shift from the run-and-shoot toward a more conventional offense. The run-and-shoot has no tight end, no fullback, four smallish receivers, a quarterback, and a running back. The trend around the league was bigger receivers—guys like Jerry Rice, Cris Carter, and Sterling Sharpe.

Getting Herman really gave us an advantage. Because of his size (6'4", 210 pounds), our quarterbacks could just throw the ball up there and let him get it. There's no question that he made our offense more versatile. Herm started slow with only 11 catches his rookie year, but by 1995 he pulled in 123, which was a league record that stood for seven years.

Another of our receivers was Brett Perriman, who despite being only 5'9", was the strongest wideout I've ever been around. This dude was a beast. He was stronger than me and most of the linemen; he could bench 500 pounds! Between Brett, Herm, and Johnnie Morton, we had all three levels of the field covered. Herman was the possession guy, Brett was our third-down, over-the-middle target, and Johnnie could just fly.

What made these guys special wasn't just their ability to catch the ball, but the pride they took in blocking was something you could feel. Other receivers would talk about making great catches, these guys would focus on springing a block. You can't protect the quarterback

Wide receiver Herman Moore, who had great size and great hands, hauls in a 17-yard touchdown pass against the Minnesota Vikings in 1996. (AP Images)

or create holes for the running back without the offensive line, but what blocking receivers did was they allowed Barry to turn a 30 or 40-yard run into 60 or 80 yards. They had as much to do with Barry's success as we did.

There's no doubt that the star of the receiving corps was Herman. Unlike some of his counterparts around the league, he kept a small circle of confidants. He didn't talk much; he was always about business. He was a good teammate while I was there. He showed up every day ready to play.

## Beware of the Backup Quarterback

It happens almost every year in the NFL; a backup quarterback fills in for a few games, looks good, and then gets overpaid by some desperate team, looking for the quarterback of the future. For the Lions it happened after the 1993 season. That year Dan Marino, the greatest Miami Dolphin of all time, ruptured his Achilles tendon in Cleveland. A relatively unknown left-hander came off the bench and made himself a ton of money.

The funny thing is that it wasn't like Scott Mitchell led Miami to some great success—the Dolphins only won three of his seven starts—but Mitchell threw 12 touchdowns in those games. He looked the part—handsome, 6'6", with a strong arm. That was enough for our general manager, Chuck Schmidt.

The Scott Mitchell era in Detroit really didn't get off to a great start.

We knew that we needed a quarterback, but it's not like the Lions were throwing money around. Hey, the best player in team history, Barry, had to fight for his money, including a holdout. But that didn't matter. These guys wanted their quarterback and set their sights on Mitchell.

So Chuck and Wayne Fontes flew out to Miami as soon as free agency started and gave him a $5 million bonus. This was for a guy who wasn't on our team and hadn't proven a damn thing in the NFL. And by the way, if a Hall of Fame coach like Don Shula is letting a young quarterback go, what does that tell you?

Talk about blatant disrespect for Barry. To see the team treat its best player that way definitely made the rest of us think about how it would be for us. Another thing that people didn't take into account was that with Mitchell being a lefty, it emphasizes the right tackle, making him the blind-side protector. The Lions had franchised me a couple of times, but now it didn't seem to matter because I was on the left side.

Guys always look to the quarterback for leadership. If he's new to the team, it's important for him to ingratiate himself. Scott never did. He was really a different cat. It turns out he was having all kinds of problems at home, and I think he also felt the pressure of his big contract. Part of that was on him, and part was on his agent. The two most pressure-packed jobs in Detroit are being the Lions quarterback or playing goalie for the Red Wings. This is a huge sports market with loyal fans, but they want performance. Scott and his agent should have known what they were getting into.

Sometimes in sports—hell—in life, people get too hung up on getting the last dollar. In retrospect maybe Scott should have taken a little less to play in an easier environment. It's not like they had to even negotiate for the money; the Lions gave it to him! Guys like Barry, myself, Jerry Ball, Chris Spielman, we had to beg for every dollar but not Scott. He definitely could have found a deal somewhere for a few less bucks and maybe he'd have been happier.

We were a hungry team. We really should have been the team of the '90s after we beat Dallas in 1991, but we always came up short. We felt like we were just a quarterback away from big things. When the Lions signed Scott, it was like he never realized what had to happen to get him there; we lost family members to create salary space.

These were guys that we went to war with, and they were gone so they could sign Scott. There's no doubt in my mind that Scott's indifference cost us a Super Bowl berth—or at the very least a playoff win—and that's all we needed.

Scott didn't have a great start in Detroit, but even when he did well, he never really won us or the fans over. Truthfully, we all thought he was kind of soft. He'd slide on fourth and 1 instead of fighting for his teammates. Rather than stand in there and take a hit, he'd throw some little sidearm dink. Think about the toughness of Brett Favre or Marino, that wasn't Scott.

If we were going to go after a quarterback, we would have been better off going after a guy who was perfect for our system, a guy who ended up in the Hall of Fame, a free agent by the name of Warren Moon.

\* \* \*

Like I said, seeing how the team pursued Scott pissed off a lot of us because of the way they treated us. The first time the Lions franchised me it was basically a leverage play. As a franchise player, the Lions would have to pay me the average of the top five linemen in all of the NFL. They didn't want to do that, and we compromised on a two-year deal.

Once that deal was complete, I was franchised once again and I was pissed. Here I was in the midst of seven consecutive Pro Bowls, and Chuck and the front office were trying to nickel and dime me. My agents, Lamont Smith and Peter Schaffer of All-Pro Sports Management, had me leave town and stay in a home in Colorado (where the agency was based). They told me they'd deal with the team and wanted to shield me from any negative feedback.

So while my holdout extended through training camp and the first game (which cost me $150,000), I had no idea how much I was being trashed back home. Eventually, I reported, but it sure seemed like the team didn't want me. They never talked about a long-term deal.

Once I got back in town, I started reading stuff, so I knew there was going to be some negativity from the fans. But when I played that first home game, you would have thought I was on the other team. When they introduced me, I actually got booed as much as Mitchell, which was pretty bad. That really hurt me.

For 90 percent of guys in the league, the only way we're going to get paid is if we win. The real superstars—guys like Barry, Emmitt Smith, Marino—they're going to get their money (though Barry did have to struggle). But if our team is 5–11, we're not going to get individual accolades, and that means we're not going to get paid. I think there was a lot of resentment toward Scott because guys on the team didn't know if he was that committed like the rest of us. And if you're not all on the same page, you ain't winning in the NFL.

**Wayne Fontes (Lions head coach):** "I told my team, 'Players win. You guys win.' I had good players, and we came close, but we were missing one part to maybe win two or three Super Bowls. You need to have respect from the players, you need to have the guy under center who's the best player; there's no question about it. The teams that win have the best quarterback that season. Go look up all the Super Bowls–the coaches who had the best quarterbacks all of a sudden were the best coaches. Teams that win have that guy."

I admire Coach for not calling Scott out specifically, but it's pretty clear who he's talking about, and he's 100 percent right. The one funny thing to come out of my contract struggle was that Scott's wife made a sign that called me and him "The Boos Brothers." This actually allowed me and him to bond. We ended up winning seven games in a row. By about the fourth game, the boos stopped for me. They never stopped for Scott.

## My "Guarantee"

One of the reasons I wanted to write this book is to clear up some misperceptions about me and some of the things I have said over the years. One incident that still bugs me is my "guarantee" for the 1995 playoff game against the Philadelphia Eagles.

That year we were sitting at 3–6 and a long shot to make the playoffs. That's when our offense just broke out. We won our last seven games, averaging 32 points per game. We entered the postseason as arguably the hottest team in the NFL. I said that if we play the way we'd *been* playing, we *should* beat the Eagles. Pretty common sense stuff. Somehow, it turned into a guarantee. It's funny, but years later, on a return flight from ESPN, I sat next to one of the editors of a Detroit newspaper sports section. He admitted that they, too, took my quote out of context and knew what I had actually said. From there it just got out of control, spreading like wildfire. This was my first real experience in being burned by the media.

Wayne, though, came out to the team, and said, "We'll back Lomas up," which was nice of him to give me that kind of support.

**Barry Sanders**: "I didn't pay attention to many guys with what they had to say in the media, but I was shocked when Lomas predicted we were going to win in Philadelphia. I was shocked. I don't know if someone baited him into saying that, but he didn't strike me as a big talker. I was shocked by that. But because he was a kind of a mentor, I just assumed he knew what he was talking about. I was like, 'Lomas doesn't necessarily go out on a limb and make waves or anything like that, so he must know what he was talking about.' I'm not a betting man, but I would have bet everything that we would have won that game."

But the Eagles took it and ran. Their coach, Ray Rhodes, pinned it up on the wall, said that I had said the Eagles sucked, that they were done. He even crazily said I "broke into their house and sodomized their wives."

It's safe to say I was not the most popular guy in Philly that week. The night before we even got to the stadium, the fans were just raucous. Outside of the stadium, they were shaking the bus, chanting, "Lo-mas, Lo-mas." I was like, "Wait, I'm an offensive lineman! And I didn't even say anything bad!"

We got to Veterans Stadium, and when I first went out, in just a T-shirt and uniform pants, it wasn't too bad. Then we came out in full uniforms for stretching, and the fans were just killing me. One 12-year-old kid was cursing like a sailor. I even asked his father if he let his son talk like that. I had no idea a seemingly innocent comment would be blown out of proportion like that. And we still had to play the game!

We lost 58–37, but that doesn't tell the whole story. Scott threw two interceptions for touchdowns, and the Eagles outscored us 31–0 *in the second quarter!* That included a Hail Mary and two Pick-6s.

**Fontes**: "We just lost that game. We played flat, didn't play very well, and that's a shame, but to say that Lomas' quote in the paper caused us to lose or caused Philly to play better—my gosh—why doesn't every team put something in the paper about the other team to make them play better? Like they say, sticks and stones break bones, but words will never hurt me. Whatever Lomas said was what he wanted to say, and I had no problem with it."

It was my last game as a Lion. Years later, I heard things, like Wayne was fed up with my "guarantee," that I was too outspoken for the organization, stuff like that. I know that nobody wants to hear athletes complain about money. But I really did have to fight and struggle to get my money with the Lions.

As a rookie I was drafted sixth, the second lineman behind Bill Fralic of the Atlanta Falcons. Russ Thomas was the general manager, and he was known as a tough negotiator. Unfortunately for me, that was the year that the United States Football League folded, so I lost some major leverage that players before me had taken advantage of. My agent was trying to get me close to Fralic's salary, but it didn't go well. I ended up holding out a couple of weeks in training camp but still made the All-Rookie team.

When I left Detroit, I was in the middle of seven straight Pro Bowls. I wasn't good enough for the Lions, but the Arizona Cardinals couldn't wait to sign me, and same goes for the New York Giants a little later. Detroit wanted to save some money, and they wanted someone quiet. Yes, I did do some talking, but you can't say that I didn't back it up.

# Chapter 7

# The Scott Mitchell Controversy

There's been a lot of talk about my quote about letting my man rush past me and hurting Scott Mitchell during a game against the Green Bay Packers in 1994. Now, we're going to set the record straight. In 2012 I was working at ESPN and doing a spot on the radio with hosts Bram Weinstein and Ryen Russillo. We were talking, and I don't know what triggered it, but that's when I said it: I let my man get by so he could sack and injure Scott Mitchell. The fact, though, is that it never happened.

I think my emotions got the best of me. I *wanted* it to be true, and your memory can be a funny thing. On the radio I even said that I told Kevin Glover I'd miss the block on purpose. And when I said it, I *thought* it was true. Here's exactly what I said: "We were getting beat 24–3 at that time, and he just stunk up the place. He's throwing interceptions, just everything. So I looked at Kevin Glover, our All-Pro center, and I said, 'Glove, that is it.' I said, 'I'm getting him out the game.'…So I got the gator arms on the guy. At the last minute, he got around me, he hit Scott Mitchell, he did something to his finger…and he came out the game…We ended up losing that game 27–24."

After the show I was truly disgusted with how I sounded. It wasn't so much the missed block as that I'd let someone get hurt. My wife heard the reaction back in Detroit and called me to ask what I had said. That's when I knew how big this was going to be. My bosses at ESPN called me in the next morning and had pulled the play in question. As we pored over the video, one thing became clear: *it never happened!*

I blocked the hell out of my guy, and another guy from the outside came blitzing. Scott never saw him, and the guy hit him on the wrist. It came from my side, but it wasn't my guy. My mouth was just open. For all those years, in my mind, I thought I had done this, but they proved me wrong. Sensitivities were running high at that time in Bristol; Rob Parker had been fired a few months earlier for making derogatory comments about Robert Griffin III being an "Uncle Tom." The last thing ESPN wanted was another public relations disaster. Management set up an apology tour, and I did the "car wash," appearing on just about every show on the network and apologized. Now they didn't tell me verbatim what to say, but they made sure I did apologize.

**Wayne Fontes (former Lions head coach):** "Lomas would never not block for anyone. That is so untrue, it's unreal...Lomas Brown has too much class for that."

As this thing was spreading like a fire out of control, I decided to call Scott. This wasn't something I was looking forward to but figured it was like a Band-Aid and that we'd just go ahead and rip it off quickly. Scott's reaction was *not* what I was expecting. Although I expected Mitchell to be hostile, he was almost jovial. I told him what had happened and gave him the entire explanation.

He said he remembered the play and knew that I hadn't let my man through. Then came the interesting part; he asked if we could continue to pretend to be mad at each other and drag the story out! His explanation was that this was the best thing that had happened to him in years. He'd never received this type of media attention. He was promoting his business, and this was perfect for it. That's when Scott went on Dan Patrick's radio show and said this:

**Scott Mitchell (former Lions quarterback)**: "It just really hurt. It was extremely disappointing. I'm really shocked by it, to be honest. Here's a guy I've had in my house. I had a big dinner for the offensive linemen every year. He came to my house and ate dinner. I gave my offensive linemen gifts every year. For him to do that is just reprehensible, beyond words. It's really disappointing, it really is painful. When you mess with my family, mess with my livelihood, mess with my health, it's unacceptable. It's B.S. I just wouldn't do it to a teammate. I wouldn't do it. If Lomas has a problem with me, come talk to me. To try to get someone hurt, it's just mind-boggling."

This whole episode tells you what type of guy Scott is. I know that if someone had said what I did on the radio, I would be pissed. Then, when it's cleared up, I certainly wouldn't try to drag things out. Something like this really makes you think. I *hope* he didn't have an agenda when he was playing, but you never know what's inside someone's head.

When we talked that night on the phone, he dumped a bunch of stuff on me, family problems, the whole deal. I wished he had shared some of that with me back in the day. We were a team, a locker room full of brothers. As a captain I would have tried to help. Scott got his money, but for a lot of guys on the team, their financial well-being depended on the team's success. Everyone had to be pulling in the same direction. If Scott had stuff that prevented him from doing so, he should have let us know.

The timing of this whole thing was not good. About a week after it happened, I was inducted into the Michigan Sports Hall of Fame.

The Lions wanted to do something to recognize my accomplishment, but we decided to let things sit while the storm passed.

Since we're clearing the air on this episode, I do want to get this out there. ESPN had no problem with what I did or the apologies. A little bit later, I was suspended for two days but that was for getting into a battle on Twitter, not the Mitchell incident. But Scott couldn't leave well enough alone. Two-and-a-half years after my comments, Scott was still complaining about it. In March of 2015, he did an interview with *Sports Illustrated*'s Monday Morning Quarterback, trying to get some more publicity.

**Mitchell**: "It just was so crushing to me. It's one thing if it is someone who has never played, but when it is your teammate and someone who understands all of what goes into games and playing they know the challenges. To take a shot like that was such a low blow, it just killed me...This was a guy I had in my own home...it was someone I bought gifts for every year, and he accepted them very graciously, someone who I always kind of thought had my back. I got booed at home games for five years every time I got introduced. It was just how it was. Lomas was the beloved player, but he held out one year, and when he finally signed, everyone was really mad at him, so people started booing Lomas. He started to understand what I was going through and he came to me and said, 'We're kind of the boos brothers.' So I thought, *this is my guy.* It just didn't make sense, but what it did was it perpetuated how people viewed me."

This whole thing is so crazy that if it didn't happen to me, I'd be laughing. Yes, we were teammates, but it was Scott who never ingratiated himself with the rest of the guys. For him to make it sound like he was one of us is really a joke. He always acted like an outsider, and that is what he was.

**Mitchell**: "Brown called me and he was very apologetic. He explained his reasoning. He said, 'I'm trying to get a better deal with ESPN. They wanted me to be more controversial.' But either way—you are going to use me and our relationship to better yourself and essentially lie—or you really meant this? My agent wanted me to sue him. There was no way I was going to do that. Can you imagine that? That would certainly take on a life of its own: former NFL quarterback sues his former lineman. But it really hurt. None of it was good, let's put it that way."

Let's set the record straight once and for all. When I talked to Scott, I was upset with my comments and apologized. But I also asked him some questions, and we talked about some of the stuff he was going through. The veterans on that team were desperate to get over the hump and thought Scott could help. But he wasn't all in, and we knew it. Did I *ever* think about letting him get hit? Hell yeah, I did. But I played for 18 years and three decades in this game. I love this game. There's no way I'd ever disrespect it by letting my own guy get hit.

**Barry Sanders (former Lions running back)**: "I knew Lomas was a great player. It was a surprise to see how it all happened, unfortunately. It doesn't change anything in my mind, am not surprised that it never actually did happen because Lomas took pride in what he did, and the players who went against him knew what type of player he was. To play this game at that position for that many years is amazing. I have the utmost respect for Lomas."

**Jay Crawford (ESPN anchor)**: "I'm happy to hear that was his recollection of it because I judge Lomas on the fabric of the man I know him to be. And I know beyond a shadow of a doubt that he would never intentionally do what he said he did. Did he think it? Maybe because he thought it, as time went on, he believed that's what he actually did. I've always hated that this happened."

**Dana Jacobson (former ESPN anchor)**: "In knowing Lomas how I do, I'm sure he wanted Mitchell out of the game. My guess at the time as a fan I probably wanted him out. I appreciate the honesty Lomas shared in talking about it years later. We say we want honesty and then we hammer people for it. I can't do that... It's a quality in Lomas I love. He wasn't going to sit there and say something he didn't believe just to make good TV or make himself look good. He's real and honest, and I will always appreciate and respect him for that."

ESPN *did* want me to be a little edgier. Just look at what they do with the likes of Skip Bayless and Stephen A. Smith. That's what sells. But I never lied to try and become that. When we found out that I had never actually let him get hit, that I blocked the hell out of my guy, it was a huge relief. I was convinced I had done this! If I was sitting around with friends, I would have sworn it to be true. So in a big way, the ESPN incident helped me be at peace with myself.

Scott Mitchell, who often struggled at quarterback for us, insisted on keeping up the ruse that I intentionally whiffed in pass blocking for him. He did that to stay in the public's eye.

**Crawford**: "There's the saying: 'The older I get, the better I was.' I think he wasn't exaggerating his skill set; he may have just gotten caught up in that. I don't really believe that he did that. I don't. Again, not having talked to him about it, maybe he did, but the guy I know would never give less than 100 percent. He'd never put a teammate in harm's way. I think the whole thing took on a life of its own. In the course of telling a story, maybe he exaggerated it a touch and embellished it just enough to raise some eyebrows to say, 'Wait, you did what?' I really thought the whole thing was unfortunate for both Scott and for Lomas because I don't think for a second that he would really do that."

In our discussion Scott dumped a lot of stuff on me like things he was going through with his family during his years in Detroit. Out of respect for his family, I won't get into them. But when you have a team full of guys, everyone goes through some stuff. I was in the middle of a divorce. But that's why they call us professionals; you leave it all behind when you take the field. If you need help, you get it. But between the white lines, you have to be there for your brothers.

So again, did I think about it? Yup, that one day against the Packers, I definitely did. But it wasn't something I sat around contemplating, and I certainly never let my own quarterback take the hit. As far as his lawyer, c'mon man! Scott told me this was the best thing that ever happened to him. He can say everything he wants, but he wanted this to go on, to put him back on the map. This is probably part of what got him on *The Biggest Loser* in 2015. I get it; we all have to find ways to make our money. That's fine but to perpetuate a lie is not cool.

# Chapter 8
# **Quarterbacks**

I've already talked in detail about Scott Mitchell, but here's my break-down/insider's take on the other Lions quarterbacks I played with.

### Eric Hipple

This is one tough hombre. Especially during our bad years, he took an absolute beating. I know that during my rookie season, my mistakes got him hit a few times. My learning experience brought him a lot of pain. But the thing about Hip is that he never complained. He was just like Barry Sanders in that way. I remember one time Tampa Bay Buccaneers linebacker Scot Brantley just crushed him, knocked his helmet right off. It was the most vicious hit I've ever seen. And Hip never uttered a word.

His real legacy has nothing to do with football. Eric's son, Jeff, took his own life back in 2000. Eric dealt with depression and got involved with drugs and alcohol. He hit rock bottom.

But Hip has come out on the other side. He's reaching out to former NFL players, helping them open up, and understand that they're not alone. He is now the outreach coordinator of the Depression Center for the University of Michigan. He was a hell of a quarterback, but what he's doing now is infinitely more important.

### Joe Ferguson

Joe was in his 13th year when he came to Detroit and he was as tough as an old piece of leather. I remember a time I was sitting on a bus behind some coaches, and Joe was across the aisle. The coach was reading a book by John Madden, and Madden was talking about Joe. I just thought that was the coolest thing. From his accomplishments I placed Joe on a pedestal. Remember, I was a huge Miami Dolphins fan during his heyday with the Buffalo Bills.

Like Eric, Joe never complained. He had seen everything and done everything. Wilber Marshall once hit him so hard that Joe was out before he even hit the ground. There wasn't a peep from our crushed quarterback. This tough guy was able to play until he was 40 years old because he worked out all the time. He was a very cool guy.

### Chuck Long

Chuck was supposed to be the next big thing for the Lions. He was the 12th pick of the 1986 NFL Draft out of the University of Iowa and finished second to Bo Jackson for the Heisman Trophy in the closest race in the history of the award. But when he came to Detroit, it just never worked. Our offense was just not good; we had no ingenuity. We were vanilla, which in our division meant he would get crushed. We played the Chicago Bears with their attacking, blitzing 46 defense twice a season. This poor guy had no shot.

### Bob Gagliano

What a great guy. I can honestly say that Bob was one of the nicest guys I've ever played with. And he was a pretty decent quarterback, too. He was a 12th-round pick, and by the time he got to Detroit, he was on his third team. He was never going to be a star, but he worked hard and filled in when we had injuries.

I, though, do have a bone to pick with Gags.

In 1989 we were playing the Pittsburgh Steelers. Bob was about to get hit, and we made eye contact. Then, to avoid the sack, he made the worst decision of his career. *He lateraled the ball to me.* Because I was behind the line, it was considered a rush. I picked up three yards but told him to *never* give me the ball again.

### Rodney Peete

I've always thought Rodney got a bum deal. Unfortunately, he was Mr. Glass; he just couldn't stay healthy. If Rodney could have stayed on his feet, he would have been awesome. He had all the tools. He had a good arm, was accurate, and could scramble. With all of his injuries, it's a wonder that he played 15 seasons! He did a great job with the Philadelphia Eagles and would have done the same thing here. I never understood why the Lions let him go. He's one of my best friends now and he and his wife, Holly Robinson-Peete, have done incredible work for autism, which affects their son. Whenever I see him, I kiddingly call him "Bucky," because while having a huge heart, my brother also has huge teeth.

### Andre Ware

I talked about Andre earlier in the book, but there is one good story to share. We had a teammate. To protect his identity, I'll call him "Joe." Well, Joe would prance around the locker room wearing nothing but an athletic supporter and a smile. Usually, he'd be glistening with some type of ointment to show off his muscles.

Dre and "Joe" were best of friends and were always hanging out together. Well, some of the guys started thinking that "Joe" might… um…well, be on the other team, if you catch my drift. He wasn't. But remember this was in the early '90s, and being gay still carried a stigma, especially in a macho environment like an NFL locker room. Things have improved on that front today. Now teams can openly accept guys like Michael Sam, and it's not even an issue.

Anyhow, we were in the middle of a three-game losing streak and decided to call a team meeting. It was a good chance to air our grievances. So we're all getting stuff off our chest and were just about done.

Talented but injury prone, quarterback Rodney Peete drops back to pass in 1993.

Except for Dre. "I just need to say something," Dre said. The room got quiet. "I just want to say, 'Joe' gets some hellacious hoes!"

Well, that cleared things up.

### Erik Kramer

For better or worse, Erik was a guy with brass you-know-what. He was unafraid to do whatever it took for the team. He was about the players. There were several times when the coaching staff would send in a play, and Erik would be like, "We're not running this, we'll do *this!*" We in the huddle loved it, but Wayne Fontes and the staff? Not so much. Wayne would run halfway out on the field and be yelling at Erik. Then later in the game, Wayne would send in a play Erik didn't like and he'd change it again.

There was a level of mistrust between players and management, and it showed itself when at times they'd make sure we didn't reach certain incentives, whether it was a specific amount of carries, catches, or whatever. If Erik knew about it, he'd change the play and help his guy get the extra cash. He was really one of the guys.

### Don Majkowski

This guy was a trip. The "Magic Man" is best known as the guy who Brett Favre replaced in Green Bay, and by the time he came to Detroit, he was at the end of the line. The funny thing is you'd never know it. Everything rolled off his shoulders. Magic's mantra was kind of: "stay calm, be happy." He's a really cool guy.

### Dave Krieg

I loved blocking for him. He is one of the more underrated quarterbacks in NFL history. He wasn't like a Marino or Montana, but when you look at yardage leaders, he's always in there. A funny footnote in the game when I "let" Scott Mitchell get hit was that Dave came off the bench and almost won the game for us.

Dave was really a mature guy, kind of like a father figure for a lot of us. By the time he came to the Lions, he had been in the league for 14 years and had seen it all. He was a calming influence for us. He was actually pretty good at scrambling, but because he had such little hands, he is also one of the all-time fumblers in the history of the game.

The reason we had a bit of a falling out traces back to when I went to Arizona. During my free-agent visit, they asked me if I thought Dave was good enough to start for the Cardinals. I basically said that it was up to them and that I didn't really feel it was my place to say. Well, it gets back to Dave that I didn't support him and it strained our relationship. I never heard anything from him, but people around him let me know he wasn't happy. The team was getting ready to sign Jake Plummer, and they ended up not re-signing Dave. Hopefully, we can mend fences soon.

# Chapter 9

# Leaving the Lions

Leaving the Lions meant leaving the Ford family, which even though I didn't have a choice, was not easy. The biggest reason is how much I admired Mr. William Ford. He was a cool dude. I always enjoyed Mr. Ford's company and wondered why he didn't come around more. One time Jerry Ball, Chris Spielman, and myself asked him. His answer taught me a valuable lesson about leadership. He said he didn't want the coaching staff looking over their shoulders.

He believed in putting people in positions of power and letting them do it. Too often today, you see companies that are micromanaged. That wasn't Mr. Ford's deal. While he kept the low profile, he let his leaders lead. Put the coaches and players out in the spotlight. A good leader does everything he or she can to put his or her people in a position to succeed. Mr. Ford put in the structure but then stepped back.

Don't get me wrong. He *loved* his Lions. He'd come around before the games to wish us luck or afterward to shake hands and offer support, but he was no Jerry Jones. You never saw him on the sideline during games or suggesting plays.

One thing about Mr. Ford that stood out to me was his loyalty. He did what he thought was right. He would never do the minimum. I think Mike Utley is a good example of that. I don't know all the specifics, but there's no doubt that he went above and beyond when it came to taking care of Mike after his injury.

To have success—either in athletics or business—you have to have some type of ego, and I'm sure Mr. Ford did. The difference between him and an owner like Jones is that he never had to talk about his success. When you think about it, the pressure of living up to his father's last name must have been just enormous. But he just rolled up his sleeves and did the family proud. I like to think of him as the lineman among NFL owners. He did his job, but he did it in anonymity.

Because of my admiration of the man, it was not easy when it came time to leave. By letting his leaders lead, there was definitely a separation when it came to players and management. We'd talk to our coaches, they would talk to the general manager or president, and then they would talk to Mr. Ford. There were just too many layers. We knew that Mr. Ford knew football, but the information he was getting was filtered through guys like Chuck Schmidt or Russ Thomas. It's like a game of telephone. By the time whatever information reached the top, it was vastly different than when it started.

Unfortunately, my departure was a good example of this. Once the team signed Scott Mitchell to be quarterback, there was a definite change in philosophy. For just about every team, the left tackle is the most important player on the offensive line. With most quarterbacks being right-handed, the left tackle protects his blind side. Because Scott was a lefty, management convinced itself that the *right* tackle was more important, so the left tackle shouldn't be paid as much. The left tackle was…me.

Once management convinced Mr. Ford that I wasn't as important as in years past, I was toast as a Lion. The fact of the matter is, though, that the whole idea was foolish. Listen, most of the best pass rushers come from the left side; it doesn't matter if the quarterback sees him coming or not, he's still going to get crushed. If you don't have that left side protected, your quarterback won't be lasting long. I think that wrong way of thinking—plus my "guarantee" in Philadelphia—gave Mr. Ford enough ammunition to let me go. That's how I became an Arizona Cardinal.

## Heading West

Let's be totally clear about one thing: I *never* wanted to leave Michigan. I had just built a huge house in 1993 in Oakland Township. My kids were in school, and I had been named the Lions' Man of the

Year two years in a row. Detroit was my home, and I desperately wanted to retire with the Lions.

The Lions were my first team. They drafted me, and hey, I still live here 30 years later. It hurt me to leave. It's something I still think about to this day. We had built a special team, then Scott Mitchell came in, and things changed. But even that disappointment didn't undo the good we did. When I got to Detroit, the Lions weren't well thought of. They weren't winning games. They were never the national game (except, of course, on Thanksgiving), no *Monday Night Football*, none of that stuff. Even with all of the problems, the fans were super—just like they are now.

When we first got here, the rookies stayed in the visitor's locker room, while the veterans stayed in the main one. We weren't allowed to come over to the "varsity" room until guys got cut. Think about that. You're a rookie, you already feel left out, your eyes are big. The older players never really helped us because they were worried about us taking their jobs. Hell, in the locker rooms, they didn't even have products for black players. Because our skin is a little more sensitive, we use special razors things like that, but there was none of it. I'm proud that we were able to change the culture. When you're part of the change and then someone tells you you've got to go, it hurts.

Having said all of that, I was mad after the team franchised me for the second time in three years and was reluctantly willing to look into free agency for the first time. There was a good aspect to being franchised: the team would have to pay me the average of the top five left tackles in the NFL. *But* it was a one-year deal with no signing bonus, so there was no security.

In swooped the Arizona Cardinals, with a three-year offer worth $9 million, $3 million of it as a signing bonus. Truthfully, I really had no desire to join a team that was essentially a mirror image of the

Lions in terms of dysfunction. As negotiations were winding down, I frantically told my agent to call Detroit to see if they'd even come close to the numbers I was offered.

Here, my agent made a major no-no. I had asked if I could listen while they were negotiating, and he let me. That was a big mistake. There can't be much worse than listening to your bosses talking about how little they value you. Schmidt said they would *possibly* consider a two-year deal with no signing bonus. It was clear that the team didn't want me. That hurt.

**Valerie (my sister):** "He was hurt because he felt he made it as a franchise-type player, that he was due that respect, and that they'd consider him that way and that he wouldn't ever be released. He thought he'd retire there, but he learned it was a business."

**Barry Sanders (Lions running back):** "I certainly didn't expect him to be gone that soon, but I know that was a decision he made. I guess the way it was told to us was that he was past his prime, and the guy played seven more years, many of those at a very high level. It was certainly sad to see him go. I knew we were losing a great player that would not be easily replaced. For selfish reasons, the guy was just one of those anchors on and off the field. Everyone respected and valued his opinion. It was a big loss."

**Kevin Glover (Lions center):** "It's extremely tough. I knew how good he was. That wasn't a position we ever needed to worry about when he was in there. A lot of people don't remember that Lomas came in and started on Day One...There's not a lot of people who could do that in the National Football League, especially in what's toughest of the toughest positions in left tackle...We had been there 11 years together, so we were very

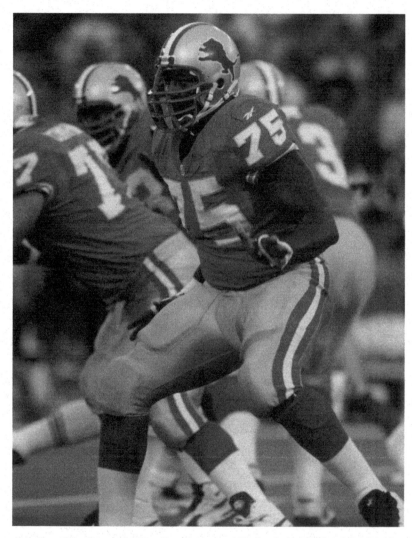

Here I am blocking during my 11-year career with the Detroit Lions. I didn't want to leave them, but they weren't interested in paying me like a player who made six straight Pro Bowls for them. (Courtesy Detroit Lions)

close. I probably missed his wife and kids more than actually missing him. We had spent a lot of time together, went to dinner a lot together; every holiday we all spent time together. So that's the part you really miss, not just the football part."

**Wayne Fontes (former Lions head coach)**: "From afar, it was like he should have died a Detroit Lion. But that's not the nature of the game. As you get older, general managers come in and say let's get someone else. But Lomas Brown was a great Lion and a great player. I can't see him in any other colors."

**Bill Keenist (Lions assistant public relations director)**: "To me, it was devastating, I love the guy. I'm just the PR guy, but I was convinced he had productive years left. But my relationship is different than the personnel department and the coaching staff. But I think in retrospect, Lomas proved to all of us that he had a lot of football left."

**Rob Rubick (former Lions tight end)**: "My reaction was, 'Why?' I didn't know if it was because he was making huge money. If the money was the same, I'd have to believe Lomas would have stayed. I didn't know why the Lions didn't pursue him harder...He still played—what, six years after that? He still had gas in the tank. He was a flexible guy. His knees were getting a little old, but he could still play. But I wasn't in the front office and don't know what happened. I'm sure they had their reasons. But as a former player, I was thinking, *Man, he's good*!...I was shocked. I thought he would be a Lion for life. I was sad. He embedded himself in the Detroit community. Even with Barry and Herman, you still thought of Lomas forever. He had done everything they asked—he had played hurt, never complained, was a leader in the locker room and the field. I won't say the Lions screwed up because I didn't know all the factors."

**Chris Spielman (Lions linebacker)**: "I don't think anyone is going to be on any team forever. The NFL is a one-day-at-a-time business when free agency and salary caps are involved. Nothing is for life."

**Sanders**: "You certainly look around and see less familiar faces. You certainly miss those guys, but that's part of the game, and you have to get used to it. But there is a strange feeling about coming in as one of the young guys, having a relationship, and growing with a group of guys, then all of a sudden seeing those guys leave. It happens, but it doesn't lessen the impact."

I was 32 years old and had made six straight Pro Bowls. This was the prime of my career. In looking back at it, I've always thought it was because of the guarantee I made before the playoff game with the Philadelphia Eagles. But like I said, I wasn't the guy who threw two Pick 6s and let a Hail Mary score before the half. That's 21 points. It's hard to come back from that. By the way, who was my replacement in Detroit? An average player named Ray Roberts, who signed for—you guessed it—a three-year, $9 million deal, the same one I got from the Cardinals.

Free agency back then wasn't like it is today, where guys change teams quickly and often. Back then, it was called "Plan B." In simple terms teams were only allowed to protect their top 37 players. As a result the guys who became free agents were often making more than those protected! It was all about supply and demand. I thought if I did leave the Lions, Philadelphia would be my new home. The Eagles were a good team, and the city was kind of a more intense version of Detroit.

I remember sitting with the relatively new owner of the team, Jeffrey Lurie. He was a little gun-shy after signing an older player the year before. He asked me, "Why should I take the risk of signing another?" Apparently my answer wasn't satisfactory, and I never went to the Eagles. At this point, it was Arizona or bust.

## Cheap Cardinals

The Cardinals were a longtime doormat and hadn't even made the playoffs since 1982. They thought they had arrived by hiring Buddy Ryan away from the Super Bowl champion Chicago Bears. The bombastic defensive genius lasted only two seasons, going 12–20 in the dessert. Let's be honest, the reason I went to Arizona was for the money. But the team did have talent. Aeneas Williams ended up going to the Hall of Fame, Larry Centers held the record for most receptions by a running back, and Eric Swann and Jamir Miller were Pro Bowlers. The potential for success was certainly there.

In the NFL there aren't a lot of secrets. Everyone pretty much knows everyone else and how they do business. Bill Bidwell was the owner of the Cardinals. His reputation was for being…well, cheap. I soon learned that this was one label that was well-earned. All the teams make money hand over fist. Between the huge TV contracts, ticket sales, and concessions, you would have to really try to run a financial loser. But Arizona left nothing to chance.

Each team has an equipment room, and it's like an open-air market for the players. We'd go in there and grab everything from T-shirts to shoes or anything else. Not in Tempe. The Cardinals' equipment room was like Fort Knox. They would give us one shirt, one pair of shorts, one pair of socks, and one athletic supporter *for the entire season*. If we wanted more, it would be deducted from our paychecks. It was easier getting stuff at the University of Florida!

I was the player rep for Arizona. Every time we went on a road trip, I'd have to fight for our per diem money. There were occasions when they'd bring us Popeye's Chicken in the locker room and then argue that we don't need per diem because they fed us. Some of the teams, like Denver, had big planes. (This was before the days of team charters.)

But Mr. Bidwell's team used a standard-sized plane. Now think about a football team with 52 huge players, plus team personnel, squeezing onto a normal-sized plane. How do you think that worked out? Even though we played out west, we were in the NFC East. That means we sometimes had consecutive road games, one week in Philadelphia, the next in Washington. And we'd travel back and forth, never just staying over in the east because it was too expensive. I had heard some of the horror stories about the Cards but had no idea how bad things were until I got there. Like I said, we had some really good players, but the penny-pinching had us focusing on that instead of the big things.

Our coach was Vince Tobin, who was about as anti-Buddy Ryan as you could get. Where Coach Ryan couldn't go more than a few minutes without speaking, Vince just kind of took everything in. He'd see everything that was going on but would sort of gather the information and wait until team meetings to share. Even during practice, he'd stand off to the side. He was kind of like Bill Belichick in the sense that he wouldn't open up to you unless you did so with him.

One thing I liked that Vince did was that he hired coaches that were as smart as he was. His offensive coordinator was Marc Trestman, while Dave McGinnis was the defensive coordinator. I thought Wayne Fontes hired coaches that wouldn't be a threat to him. Coach Tobin didn't worry about that.

I liked Coach Tobin a great deal. He introduced me to one of my all-time favorite players, the NFL's all-time leading rusher, Walter Payton. That was a big deal. I had played against "Sweetness" for a few years, and let me tell you how much respect I had for him. When our defense was on the field, that was the line's chance to catch our breath, get oxygen, rehydrate, or go over plays. When the Chicago Bears were on offense, I'd just stand there and watch—always amazed at Payton's abilities. Seeing Walter was like that. When Vince introduced us, I don't even remember what I said, but it wasn't much, I can tell you that. Payton spoke to us a few times, talking about how he trained and about his legendary running up hills. It was incredible.

Once you get to the NFL, there are times when you're just in awe. Playing against a guy like Walter was like that. When we played Dallas for the first time, I was amazed at how the star on their helmet looked three times the size I saw on TV. But you quickly realize that things are different in person.

One of the first times we played the Cowboys, it was just crazy, the stars were bigger, the blues brighter. Then, during a timeout, Hall of Famer Randy White started cussing me out. I thought maybe there was something wrong with him because this guy was crazy. He told me how I sucked, my mother sucked. Yup, these were not the Cowboys on TV.

We had some pretty good success in Arizona, much more than the Cardinals had experienced since leaving St. Louis. The highlight definitely came in the 1998 season. In Week 9 we played in Detroit. You'd better believe I had that one circled on my calendar. We won 17–15, and the guys gave me the game ball. That was one game I'll never forget.

The bigger part of that year was that we won the last three games just to qualify for the playoffs with a 9–7 record. In the first round of the playoffs, we had to take on Troy Aikman, Emmitt Smith, Michael Irvin, and the former world champion Cowboys. We might have been seven-point underdogs, but we went into Big D and just whacked them. Jake Plummer threw two touchdowns, and we rolled to an easy 20–7 victory.

For me, it was almost standard operating procedure. During my career, no matter which team I played on, we beat the Cowboys. I think overall, I lost to Dallas one time in my 18 years. On the other side, we always seemed to lose to Tampa. No matter how bad they were, the Bucs always killed my teams.

# Chapter 10

# From Cleveland to New York

We had a good thing going in Arizona, but as usual, finances got in the way. The team's general manager, Rod Graves, told me that the team wanted to keep me, but he didn't anticipate me getting a big offer. In Cleveland they were restarting the Browns franchise and didn't have a salary cap to worry about when stocking their team. Combine that with the Cardinals' tightness with a dollar, and it's easy to see how I ended up in Cleveland. The Browns went all-in and signed both me and my Cardinals teammate Jamir Miller to big contracts. (Mine was for three years and $10 million.) The other issue had to do with my family.

Everything for me is about family. I was going through a divorce, and my three girls, who were 15, 13, and 12, were all living with their mother in Michigan. Cleveland was certainly closer than Arizona and as close as I could get to Detroit. My girls took the divorce hard and didn't talk to me for a while. When I was in Arizona, my heart was still with my family. I kept my watch on East Coast time, but it still seemed like me and the girls were always missing each other. Plus, with three girls, I think it's important for them to have a positive male role model. In addition, I was dating a woman in Michigan, who is now my wife. My parents were having some health issues, so I needed to get back this way.

Another reason I chose Cleveland was that I was convinced that they would be a decent team. They had that unlimited salary cap, they had the No. 1 overall pick—Tim Couch—and some good guys on the coaching staff, guys like Ken Wisenhunt and Tony Sparano, who both went on to become head coaches. One of the major problems was at the top. Chris Palmer had been a long-time assistant, and this was his first head coaching job. To give a rookie an expansion team was not a good idea. Like a lot of first-time coaches, Palmer wanted to prove that he knew everything. I think it's the insecurity of being new and showing everyone that you deserve the job. He never listened to anyone, and while he talked about an open-door policy, it still was a waste of time trying to communicate to him.

We lost our first game 43–0 to the rival Pittsburgh Steelers, and things didn't get a whole lot better. The season started with seven straight losses before we finally won in New Orleans against the Saints. We finished 2–14. My season ended in Week 10. I got hurt on a weird play. Jim Pyne (who ironically had come over from the Lions) lined up next to me for the Browns. On a fluke play, Jim cut me, and I was out for the season.

Then things got worse.

Our right guard was a guy named Scott Rehberg, a third-year guy out of Central Michigan. He was huge (6'8", 325 pounds), but he was not mentally tough. Before a game I heard him calling his wife or fiancée saying that he had got sick the night before and wouldn't be able to play. My mouth dropped. *This is the NFL!* You *have* to try and play. If you're not getting taken out on a stretcher, then you *must* give it a shot.

Once, when I was with the Cardinals, I had a kidney stone. I'm not sure if you've ever had one, but it is painful. And no matter what, I couldn't pass the sucker. On Friday night the doctors put a catheter in me. They said that was the only way I'd be able to play. That Sunday, I was blocking Ray Lewis, Tony Siragusa, and Sam Adams of the Baltimore Ravens in a meaningless game because that's what football players do.

The only way to pass a stone is to pee it out. So they kept giving me fluids, and every time we came off the field, my teammates surrounded me, holding towels up, so I could go to the bathroom in "private." When the game was over, the doctors pulled the catheter out of me, and I actually passed out for a second.

So you can understand why when I heard Scott on the phone, I just lost it. After the game reporters asked me my opinion, and I shared it. That week Coach Palmer called me into his office and told me how I should've kept quiet and let the coaching staff deal with it. He fined me for conduct detrimental to the team.

Later that week, we had a team meeting. Coach Palmer was up there talking, and I'm biting my tongue trying not to say anything. Then he started going on about how he had to fine someone for talking about a teammate, but he never used my name. That was my breaking point.

I raised my hand and then stood up. "All you guys who don't know who he's talking about," I said, "it's me." Then I went off about Coach, and his "my way or the highway" attitude, things like that. Next thing I know, Corey Fuller and "Zeus" (Orlando Brown) both chimed in and agreed with what I was saying.

At the first day of minicamp, I knew it wasn't a good fit and I had made a mistake. This was my 15th year in the league. I was the oldest guy on the team, and guys used to come up to me all the time, asking for advice. I had to be honest with them, telling them that most teams in the league aren't like this. Coaches normally work with you, not dictate policy. All the reporters would come to me, knowing I wasn't afraid to speak my mind.

One day, Mary Kay Kabot of *The Cleveland Plain-Dealer* called me up. I'd known Mary Kay for years, and we had a great relationship. She told me that she'd spoken with management, and they didn't know if they were going to pick up my option for the next season. I still hadn't heard anything from the team, but I knew she was right.

A week later I was on my way to see my family in Detroit when Palmer called me. He gave me the whole thing about going in another direction, that I was too much of a locker room lawyer, and some other stuff I don't remember. This was not a surprise. Still, it was the first time that I'd ever been cut, and it was devastating. You know it's coming, but when you hear the words, you're never quite ready for it.

At that point, I was basically resigned to retiring. I'd played 15 years and made seven Pro Bowls. It had been a great ride. My retirement lasted about 10 minutes. My phone rang, and it was Jim Fassel of the New York Giants. (I knew him from Arizona, where he had given me a tongue lashing.) He didn't beat around the bush. He said, "I want you to come here." I resisted, but we made a deal. He asked me to come for a visit, and then I could make a decision.

The Giants were a first-class operation. The ownership with Mr. Wellington Mara, the general manager (at the time) Ernie Accorsi, the coaching staff, everyone treated me with respect. There was great history with Lawrence Taylor, Phil Simms, and Bill Parcells. Talk about a night and day change from where I'd been. Coach Fassel had some good pieces—Kerry Collins at quarterback, Tiki Barber and Rod Dayne at running back, Jessie Armstead, Keith Hamilton, Jason Sehorn, and Michael Strahan on defense. The one thing the team needed was a left tackle. They had drafted Luke Petitgout in 1999, but he couldn't handle the position, so they moved him to the right side. I was so blown away by the team's presentation, I signed right on the spot.

## Big Fun in the Big Apple

I knew the Giants were a good team, but never in my wildest dreams did I think we would go to the Super Bowl. Coach Fassel and Accorsi had a definite plan they were following in putting the 2000 squad together. One of the most important and one of the last parts to come together was the offensive line. That's where free agency came in. In addition to myself, the team signed Dusty Ziegler from the Buffalo Bills to play center, and former Bill and Kansas City Chief Glenn Parker to play guard. We all came in and started.

People talk about the pressure of playing in New York, and it *is* intense, but there's no place better. Even with the Yankees, Knicks, etc., there's no doubt in my mind that the Giants are *the* team in the city. We were playing the Philadelphia Eagles, and I'm trying to block Hugh Douglas, and my back just tightened up. I fell to the ground like a ton of bricks. While I was on the ground, the whole stadium started chanting my name. Remember, this is not a long-time Giant like L.T. or a quarterback like Collins lying on the field; this is an offensive lineman in his first year with the team! The reaction literally sent chills down my spine. It showed how well the fans knew the game. It was really one of the most uplifting moments in my entire career.

We started off with three straight wins, and all was good. We were 7–2 when we fell to the St. Louis Rams, as the defense just imploded. Trent Green threw four touchdowns and ran for another, and we lost 38–24. The week before Thanksgiving, we played the Lions! Charlie Batch threw three touchdowns, and Detroit won 31–21. After the game Chuck Schmidt came up to congratulate me, and all I could think about was, *Hey, I could have still been in Detroit!*

It was after that game that Coach Fassel made a statement that would change everything.

The Giants were 7–4 and teetering on the edge. Fassel was in danger of losing his job. That's when he said it: "We are in a five-game season right now, and that's the way I'm defining it," he said. "I am driving the train…This is a horse race, and we're coming around the far turn, and I see the finish line. This is a poker game. I'm shoving my chips to the middle of the table. I'm raising the ante."

In case there was any question, Coach made it clear: *This team is going to the playoffs. This team's going to the playoffs. I'm going to define where we're going. I'm not afraid to say one thing: we're going to the playoffs.* After the press conference, he pulled some of the veterans—me, Jessie Armstead, Barber, Collins, and Hamilton—into his office to tell us the exact same thing. We were going to the playoffs, and it was all on us to back up his words.

I'm not going to lie. We thought he was nuts. First, I thought he was crazy just to say this to the media. Then I *really* thought he had gone off the deep end when he gave us all the responsibility. It turned out he was teetering on being a crazed motivational genius. As a coach, you can only play the guarantee card one time. By putting it on us, we had ownership in it. As a team we were stuck. There's no way we should have let the Lions beat us like that at home. Coach knew we had the talent and knew we should have been better.

Whatever the reason, we took off, winning at the Arizona Cardinals and Washington Redskins, then beating Pittsburgh at home. We won a close one at the Dallas Cowboys and then closed at home with a division-clinching win over the Jacksonville Jaguars.

### The Perfect Game and the Super Bowl

That last win against the Jaguars gave us a 12–4 record and home-field advantage throughout the playoffs. This came in handy, as we dispatched Philly in the first round. Next up was the explosive

Minnesota Vikings in the NFC Championship Game. The Vikings brought in the second highest-scoring offense in the NFC. (Nobody was coming close to the "Greatest Show on Turf" Rams.) The offense looked like a Pro Bowl roster: Daunte Culpepper under center, Robert Smith in the backfield, and Randy Moss and Cris Carter as wideouts. Hall of Famer John Randle led a good defense. We were going to have our hands full—or so we thought.

Because we were home, we kicked off as 4.5-point favorites. Sure we wanted to get to the Super Bowl, but there was a little extra motivation as well. We got word that the Vikings had made up shirts that they were the NFC champions. That pissed us off. We pinned up one of those shirts and saw it before practice every day. We were *ready.* Less than two minutes into the game, Kerry hit Ike Hilliard for a 46-yard touchdown, and it was over. Our line was playing so well that they had no chance. Kerry had all day back there and threw five touchdowns. We thought we could win, but we certainly didn't foresee 41–0!

After 16 long, hard years, it was happening! I kept bouncing around on the sideline, saying, "I can't believe I'm going to the Super Bowl!" As I look back, I probably appreciated the fact that we were going to the Super Bowl more than the actual Super Bowl itself.

After spending my whole career working so hard to try and get to the Super Bowl, I can't put into words how disappointing the experience was. I still don't know what happened.

Here we were, coming off one of the most dominant NFC Championship Games in the history of the sport. On the other end of the field were the Ravens, one of the great defenses of all-time, but with no offense at all. We liked our chances. Our team was full of veterans. We knew what it took for us to get there. Everyone followed curfew, and we truly thought we were doing everything right.

I work on drills during the 2000 training camp with the New York Giants. We would reach the Super Bowl at the end of that season. (AP Images)

We had played the Ravens in preseason but had no idea how good they would be.

As a group, this was our first time going to the big game. The Ravens had never gone either. But for whatever reason, they were calmer and handled things better. Nothing seemed to faze them. Everything is bigger at the Super Bowl. Even the tickets were like three times the normal size. I made $20,000 off my tickets. Each player gets his own car. I did try to take a moment to appreciate everything. Media Day was probably the biggest aha moment, taking photos with the Super Bowl logo behind us. *Wow, this is the pinnacle of our profession, and I never thought I'd get there.* And for the game to be in Tampa, just a three-hour drive from where I grew up—well, that seemed like fate. My dad was sick, but both parents were able to come, which was huge for me, since they had only missed one college game. This was a perfect storm—until the game started.

There was no question that Baltimore was the better team that day. They played well and were more physical. After Duane Starks picked off Kerry and took it to the house, it was 17–0. Even when we had our only real sign of life—Ron Dixon returned the ensuing kickoff 97 yards for the touchdown—Jermaine Lewis took back the *next* ensuing kickoff for an 84-yard score, and that was that. You could see just by watching that we weren't right. It was like something from above.

To this day, I still haven't watched a tape of that game. My friends say I was running up and down the sideline trying to motivate my teammates. It's all a blur to me. I almost broke down crying at the end of the game. I could barely walk off the field. My linemate Parker had lost four straight Super Bowls with the Buffalo Bills. He told me before the game that losing the Super Bowl is the worst feeling ever, the most excruciating pain. He was 1,000 percent right. After the game, they throw a party for both teams, but there was no way I was going to that one.

## September 11, 2001

My second year in New York was nowhere near as good as my first. After losing our first game in Denver, we all learned how insignificant football really was. We lost on *Monday Night Football* to the

Broncos 31–20. The date was September 10, 2001. It was a long flight home, and as we'd later learn, when we landed at 6:00 AM, the hijackers were in the airport at that time. A couple of guys, including Ron Dayne, came by to my room at the Extended Stay. We were just hanging out, trying to wind down after a disappointing start of the season. The guys left at about 8:00 AM.

I was watching TV, checking out some ESPN, when all of the sudden, the all-sports network went into news mode. The first plane had struck the World Trade Center. Of course, at that point, nobody knew what was going on. We all thought it might just be an accident. I don't think there was anyone who knew the impact of what was going on. I went to the window because there was a good view of the World Trade Center. I couldn't see the actual plane—just a lot of smoke. Then the second plane hit, and I saw both towers collapse. It was like the entire city disappeared. There was smoke everywhere. I tried to call my family, but the phone lines were dead. It was the most eerie feeling I've ever had. And the smell of the gas, the buildings—and yes—the bodies, was something that was really indescribable. It was the worst odor I've ever smelled.

As the week went on, a bunch of guys went down to Ground Zero, but I just couldn't bring myself to go. There was so much destruction, I couldn't really grasp the totality of the situation. Guys were just furious that we had to practice with that stench still in the air, furious that the NFL was going to actually play the week of the biggest tragedy any of us had ever witnessed. Football really didn't matter, and we didn't feel like playing. It was weird. Normally, there would be planes flying non-stop over our practice facility. This week there was nothing. They brought a bunch of kids and spouses of firefighters to practice, probably like 100 people in all. We had crisis management experts come and talk to us, tell us what we shouldn't say, things like that. Everyone knew someone who suffered as a result of this terrorist act; we were all affected.

Fortunately, the NFL finally came to their senses and canceled all games for the week.

We resumed play the next week in Kansas City. The support we got was awesome. Chiefs fans actually gave us a standing ovation. One of my biggest regrets, though, was during the national anthem. It was so emotional that guys were tearing up left and right. But I wouldn't allow myself to cry because I thought it would make me look weak. I mean, all these people lost someone, the nation was in mourning, and I wouldn't let myself break down. I'm ashamed of that. We did do a poster with the fire department and the New York Jets, so I was proud to help a little bit, but it wasn't enough.

* * *

After the Super Bowl loss, the Giants re-did my contract to lessen their salary cap. I still got paid the same, but on paper it was listed as a seven-year deal. This is still a pretty common practice in the NFL.

There's no doubt that my play slipped a little bit in that second year in New York. I was 37 years old, but I felt like I still had some good football left in me. Looking back, one big factor in my decline was fatigue. The Super Bowl run was obviously the latest I had ever played in a season. (The last game was on January 28.) And we were back at it in April for organized team activities. My legs were shot. Even as the next year began, I was still trying to get my legs under me from the season before. It wasn't as much about getting old; it was that my body was just tired.

A lot of times when your team rides a crest of emotion, like we did with the Lions after Mike Utley's injury, or like we did with the

Giants after Coach Fassel's guarantee, it's really hard to replicate that success the next season. That was the case with us. We lost five of our last seven games to finish at 7–9.

The Giants let me know I wasn't coming back the next season, but I had bigger issues. My parents' health had really started to deteriorate. Family always has been and will be the first priority for me, so I spent a lot of time taking care of them. I tried to stay in shape, but my workouts were really more cosmetic than to get in NFL shape. I wasn't thinking about retiring but also didn't spend much time thinking about playing either.

In March, the Tampa Bay Buccaneers asked me to come down to visit, and check out their program. The Bucs were in the middle of arguably the best period in franchise history with three straight playoff appearances. But after finishing 9–7 and losing in the wild-card round for the second consecutive year, owner Malcom Glazer fired head coach Tony Dungy. Coach Dungy is a great man, and he eventually led Peyton Manning and the Indianapolis Colts to two Super Bowls, including one championship. The Glazer family, though, felt like the team needed some fire and they made a trade to hire Jon Gruden from the Oakland Raiders. After my initial visit, I waited to hear back from Tampa. Gruden had hired Bill Muir to coach the offensive line. Coach Muir was my first line coach in Detroit, and I was excited about the chance to reconnect.

# Chapter 11
# **Winning a Ring**

A day or two before training camp opened, the Bucs called, and I was heading to Tampa. I was signed with the intention of being the starting left tackle. Coach Bill Muir wanted me to be a veteran leader on a young line. But things worked out a little bit differently than anticipated.

**Jon Gruden (Buccaneers head coach)**: "We had Kenyatta Walker at left tackle when I became the head coach. I didn't think he was going to be the left tackle like he had on the previous staff. So we moved Kenyatta to right tackle, and we acquired Roman Oben, who had played for the New York Giants. When Lomas became available, it was late in his career. Bill Muir loved Lomas like all offensive line coaches did...I had a lot of respect for Lomas because I knew a little bit about him from his Gators days. I just knew bringing him back to Tampa for my first year with the Bucs that he could not only help mentor Kenyatta, but he could also be a swing tackle, and if we needed to use him as our left tackle, he could do that. And I knew he could learn the offense because we were going to ask a lot of the tackles."

**Bill Muir (Buccaneers offensive line coach)**: "Because of Lomas' background, I thought he had a little juice left in the lemon. Without using the term negatively, I thought he would be a 'stopgap' player. We weren't convinced that Roman Oben was healthy, and honestly, how good he would play. I knew that Lomas would step in and allow us to stay competitive. If Roman needed a break, Lomas would be able to step in without much of a drop-off. It was a risk worth taking. It was [Gruden and] my first year there, I wanted a positive influence in the locker room. He knew how to win, what it took to win. With young players he would take them under his wing. I wasn't sure if they knew how to be professionals. He filled those roles."

I was signed so late that I never even made the media guide. Because I had missed the organized team activities, minicamps, and lifting sessions, I wasn't in football shape and didn't know the playbook. Coach Gruden likes to run the West Coast Offense, which can be tough to pick up. Couple that with the fact the team's offseason acquisition at left tackle, Roman Oben was coming off of his best season, it soon became obvious that I wasn't going to be playing much.

That year in Tampa was without question the toughest training camp I'd ever been through. We worked out at Disney World. The heat was just unbearable, and I was still trying to get into shape. I've only called my mother twice about football problems. The first was in my early days at the University of Florida, and I wasn't sure I wanted to stay. The guys were too big and strong, and I didn't know if I belonged. The second was during this training camp. I'm a Florida guy, and this was the most draining heat I've ever felt. It took me 30 minutes to get to practice every day. I was trying to play catch-up with the playbook. I thought I had made a big mistake. Fortunately, as she did in college, Mom told me to stay and live up to my commitment. I'm so grateful that Mom straightened me out both times. If I'd have quit and the Buccaneers won the Super Bowl without me, I would have regretted it for the rest of my life.

Coaches Gruden and Muir still wanted me around to mentor the line. This team had an incredible defense led by Hall of Famers Warren Sapp and Derrick Brooks along with John Lynch and Ronde Barber, who might join them in Canton. The problem was that as good as the D was, the offensive line had no idea how to practice.

That's where I came in.

Even though I did want to get out on the field, I decided to be the best guy on the practice team, so the defense would have a good look at what they're up against. Before every practice I'd high-five Gruden. He was so full of energy, I had to match it. Defensive line coach (and future head coach of the Lions) Rod Marinelli told me I was the best practice player he had ever seen.

**Muir**: "I had no doubt in my mind that he would have a positive impact on the team, no matter what role was assigned to him. Frankly, I thought he would play a bit more than he did...but I recognized, as everyone else did, how prideful he was on the scout team. Let me tell you, there are two guys on the defense who are in the Hall of Fame [Sapp and Brooks], and there probably should be a third [John Lynch], and those guys really benefitted from the fact that Lomas Brown gave them such a great look on the scout team and encouraged other players to do the same. We had a defensive end [Simeon Rice] who was second in the league in sacks. Obviously he had great talent, but he went against Lomas Brown in practice every day, and that brought out the best he had."

**Gruden**: "Lomas did everything with a bounce in his step and to the best of his abilities, whether he was on the PAT/field goal team, the kickoff return team. He was on the scout team. He set a real good tone as one of the truly great veteran leaders I've been around. I don't know how many guys would have done that. It's a credit to him."

Truthfully, it's incredible for me to think that we won a Super Bowl with that line. Our center was only 250 pounds (Jeff Christy). Oben (a former first-round disappointment with the Giants) played left tackle, and undrafted journeyman Kerry Jenkins was the left guard. The right side was Kenyatta Walker, a highly touted, but overhyped second-year player out of Florida, and Cosey Coleman, who had bad knees. Our offensive line was one of the worst practicing, laziest groups I'd ever seen. But in fairness, they didn't know any better. My job was to teach.

**Muir**: "I think what Lomas was referring to was the young players, and there were several of them that we were counting on, and those were the guys that needed to have a change in attitude, and they did. I would call that the Lomas Brown Effect."

**Gruden**: "There was a lot of work that needed to be done. That's why we made a lot of changes on the line. We moved Kenyatta from left to right tackle, we brought in Oben, brought in Brown, brought in Kerry Jenkins and a number of other linemen."

I didn't really know how to practice until my first Pro Bowl. Jackie Slater, the Hall of Fame right tackle of the Los Angeles Rams, was 36 years old but running all over the field. I went up to him amazed and asked if that's how he always worked, and he said you practice how you play. It was a pretty simple answer, but it always stuck with me.

In football it's an unwritten rule that you pass on your knowledge to the next guy, and that's how you make a mark on the game. The Tampa offensive linemen had never seen anything like that. Simeon Rice and I were reunited in Florida. We had been teammates with the Arizona Cardinals and we had some epic practice battles. He was a Pro Bowl defensive end, who finished his career with 122 sacks. It was great to renew our practice matchups every day. That is what we had to teach the Bucs.

Looking back at the year, it was really something I ended up enjoying. Coach Gruden took care of me. He easily could have (sometimes maybe *should* have) deactivated me, but instead he carried me for field goal protection. He did that because he respected me, and I'll never forget that. It was because of the way I practiced.

**Gruden:** "He's a pro, we're going to play the best players. It's not like we wanted to keep anybody on the bench or just play the young guys. We weren't playing any brain games. We felt Oben was the best LT we had, but we still had a big role for Lomas as a swing tackle and a man who could help us on and off the field in developing our program, and I give him a lot of credit for that, checking his ego at the door. That's what makes him real special in my heart forever."

The closest I got to "real" playing time was Week 5 in Atlanta. Roman was struggling, and Coach Muir told me to stretch. Here I was, in my 18th year, and I'm stretching on the sideline and filled with butterflies! Roman improved, and I never got in. The experience in Tampa gave me a whole new appreciation for what backups go through. They have to practice like a starter and be ready both physically and mentally, yet their time might never come. When I was the starter, I was so zoned in that I only worried about the next play. As a reserve I had to fight things like looking into the stands and having my focus drift.

## Coach Gruden

Playing for Gruden was a terrific experience. He treated me with respect, and even after I retired, I learned how highly he spoke about me and my time in Tampa. These days, you watch Jon on *Monday Night Football*, and you think he's half-crazy. He is *so* intense, so into the game. Nobody could really be that enthusiastic. But that is the same Jon Gruden I played for.

Coming to Tampa was a little weird because I was actually older than the coach. Because of that I think that we hit it off so well. We'd been in the NFL for about the same amount of time and we were chasing the same thing. We had our own unspoken language.

Gruden is one of the most intense people I've ever met—in or out of football. Just about all football coaches curse, but there are certain words they won't use. Jon had no such list. It took a special breed to be able to play quarterback for him. We were lucky that our team could handle the heat. This was a coach who was involved with everything, especially the offensive line and quarterbacks. And he wasn't shy about expressing his opinions.

Nothing got Brad Johnson too up or too down. This dude was on an even keel—perfect for a quarterback under Gruden. A Pro Bowler like Keyshawn Johnson couldn't take it, and eventually he'd be shipped out of town. Keenan McCardell may not have been as talented as Key, but he could deal with "Chucky," so he flourished. Shaun King showed some ability as a young quarterback, but Gruden was overbearing for him, and he went from starter to backup really quick. Same thing happened with Rob Johnson, a laid-back guy. Coach Gruden wasn't for everyone, but he was smart in the way he built his team—from the veterans on out.

I give the Glazer family a lot of credit for making the move to fire Tony Dungy. Don't get me wrong, he was a great coach; but it was obvious the Bucs had pretty much plateaued. Tony is a laid-back, religious guy, and Tampa Bay needed someone who would shake things up. That was Coach Gruden.

\* \* \*

Even if I was going to spend the year basically on the sideline for Gruden, make no mistake, I wanted that championship ring. And I picked a good team to try and get it with.

The 2002 Bucs were far from an offensive juggernaut. Brad Johnson did a nice job at quarterback, Keyshawn Johnson was still a very good wide receiver, and Mike Alstott was a monster at fullback. But this team would live and die with its defense. Our guys held opponents to about 12 points per game, the best in the NFL. It wasn't usually pretty, but we mauled our way to five wins in the first six games en route to a 12–4 season.

In our first playoff game, we beat up San Francisco, holding the 49ers to 62 yards rushing and picked off Jeff Garcia three times. Brad threw a couple of touchdowns, and we rolled 31–6. The NFC Championship Game was in Philadelphia. I really shouldn't have been surprised, as the Eagles and I crossed paths over and over. It all started when I thought they might draft me coming out of college. My last game as a Lion was the "guarantee" game, when the fans chanted my name and rocked our bus. I'd been back there with the Giants, and let's just say that the fans never forgot who I was or what I allegedly had guaranteed. For me to get back to the Super Bowl, of course, it had to go through the City of Brotherly Love. You'd think the fans would ignore me since I wasn't really playing, but you'd be wrong. They never forgot anything. This was the last game at Veterans Stadium, and two 12–4 teams were playing for the right to go to the big game. How sweet would it be to shut that place down?

The Eagles were very good. Donovan McNabb led an offense that included fellow Pro Bowler Chad Lewis at tight end and 1,000-yard rusher Duce Staley in the backfield. Defensively, they weren't as good as us, but they could almost field their own Pro Bowl team with defensive end Hugh Douglas, cornerbacks Bobby Taylor and Troy Vincent, and safety Brian Dawkins all making the trip to Hawaii. It was no surprise that they were favored by four points.

Our defense was unreal that day, allowing one touchdown and one field goal. We dominated the game but still only led 20–10 with about three-and-a-half minutes to go. That's when Barber picked off McNabb and took it 92 yards to the house. It was time for the Vet to close down. We were heading to San Diego, to get me that Super Bowl ring!

The Oakland Raiders popped the Tennessee Titans in the AFC Championship Game to set up a dream matchup: Gruden's new team taking on his old team. Oakland had as many big names as you could find. Journeyman quarterback Rich Gannon was the league's MVP, and they had future Hall of Famers Jerry Rice, Tim Brown, and Rod Woodson.

The funny thing is that other than Coach Gruden, we were definitely the "other" team for the whole week. Offense sells, and the Raiders had all the big names. They had a huge offensive line. Everyone thought they were going to win their fourth Super Bowl and they were a 3.5-point favorite. And you know what? If they had played anyone besides us, they might have pulled it off. But we had a great defense, and we had the biggest difference in the game—Gruden.

No team I'd ever been on was more prepared than we were for that game. Yeah, they had a new head coach, but much of the staff was the same, and we knew *everything* about them. Your team is your team, and you can't really change that much. There was nothing in their playbook that was going to surprise us.

The day before the game, the Raiders were dealing with something totally unexpected. All-Pro center Barret Robbins went missing. He returned that night but was so out of it that the team deactivated him for the Super Bowl. Robbins had been dealing with depression and didn't take his medication. (He would be diagnosed with bipolar depression and later tested positive for steroids.) It's easy to say the Raiders were distracted, and we'll never know. What I do know is that it was almost a distraction for us. It was such a big mystery that we had no idea what was going on.

Once the game started, I knew Oakland didn't have a chance. They kicked an early field goal to make it 3–0, and that was about it. We scored 34 unanswered points and did it in all kinds of different ways— a couple of field goals, an Alstott touchdown, a couple of touchdowns to Keenan, and then Dwight Smith picked off Gannon and took it 44 yards to the house. This thing was *over*. By the time Brooks ran back another Gannon pick, who threw five, it was 41–21. Dwight got *another* Pick-6 with just two seconds left, and we were world champions 48–21.

As much as a rout as my first Super Bowl had been, this was the total opposite. We knew everything that was coming and just crushed the Raiders. After 18 long years, I was finally a champion! I had never won a title in high school, and Florida's SEC crown was taken away. This was my first time being on top of the world, and it was awesome.

All the confetti started to fall, and unlike with the New York Giants, this time it was *my* team's color. My parents were in the stands, and it was everything I could ever ask for. We all got to take pictures. I kissed the Lombardi Trophy. It was even sweeter than I anticipated.

You hear a lot of guys say how they dreamed about winning the Super Bowl. I never did. This was kind of a strange way to win one, not starting, never getting my uniform dirty, but I kind of looked at it as a lifetime achievement award. I had paid my dues and now I was a champion.

I also thought about all of those great guys I played with—guys like Barry Sanders, Kevin Glover, Mike Utley. I was probably the last guy still playing. When I got to Detroit, Jerry Ball, Glove, and I would sit around, talking about the Super Bowl. I had made a vow that I'd never go unless I was playing. And now I won the championship—won it for all of my guys.

My wife, Wendy, and I celebrate winning Super Bowl XXXVII with the Tampa Bay Buccaneers. (Courtesy Lomas Brown)

**Chris Spielman (former Lions linebacker)**: "For guys I didn't play with, I was envious. For guys I did play with, I smiled because I know their personal story. It's like if you watch your kids play sports, and you're in the stands. When they have success, you're much happier than they actually are. Seeing Lomas win that Super Bowl, it's a huge attaboy."

**Barry Sanders (former Lions running back)**: "I was thrilled for him and I did feel a part of that to some degree through my relationship with him and I did take some pride in that. He was one of my closest guys from the game. He meant so much to my career that I did take some satisfaction in his experiences in the Super Bowl. That's the guy Lomas is. I remember him telling me that, and that says a lot about him, that he was thinking about some of his earlier teammates, that he hadn't forgotten, and we were in some way significant. He made us a part of that. That's what type of guy he is."

**Kevin Glover (former Lions center)**: "Most people think you would be jealous or disappointed you weren't in that situation. When you care for your teammates and friends, you're pleased that they reached those goals. You're happy because you know what kind of person they are and what type of hard work they put in to accomplish their goals. I know the long road it took him to get there, and he left after our 11th year...He won it in his 18th year. That's a long time to stay true to your craft and the work it takes to stay on top of your game."

**Mike Utley (former Lions lineman)**: "It was great! I mean 75—that was Big Daddy! I'm glad for him...I think it's the coolest thing in the world. There can only be one No. 1, and I'm so glad that that year, at that time, Lomas was that person, that left tackle who was No. 1. It was like, 'Okay, the next time we see each other, he's buying the margarita!'"

**Muir**: "Outside of the pride and the joy I felt in my heart for winning that game, it was an equal amount of pride because I was able to get Lomas a ring. People will have great careers, and they'll finish without a ring, and that will be a missing part of their career. I was so happy that Lomas was able to put a Super Bowl ring on his finger, regardless of whether he was going to play again or not, I just felt very good about him being on the team and being able to put that ring on."

**Gruden**: "It was very important for me to get him that ring. You think about the great players who have had storied careers and never won a championship, you think of Karl Malone, John Stockton, Dan Marino...To see one of the truly great players in professional football get his time, get his ring, I think that ring represents more than a championship. I think it represents his body of work."

And I'm not going to lie, I thought about my miserable year in Cleveland, and Coach Palmer telling me the team was cutting me, the Super Bowl loss with the New York Giants, and how much that hurt. It was a blessing to sign with Tampa, especially considering how close I came to leaving. I wish every player would have the experience of winning the Super Bowl. Once you experience something like that, it's something that will motivate you for the rest of your career, the rest of your life. To see all your work pay off, it's reflecting on your whole life. I look at some of the great linemen who never got to hoist the Lombardi Trophy—Slater, Bruce Matthews, Chris Hinton—and yes, I'd have to say that I'd feel unfulfilled had I not gotten that taste.

## The Retirement Dilemma

After finally climbing the mountain, I still wanted to play. I had in some ways taken the year off, and my body felt great. On the bus after the Super Bowl, Coach Gruden told me how much he loved me and told me that he wanted to sign me to a two-year contract right on the spot. I knew it was the adrenaline talking. We had just won the championship, and everyone loved everyone else.

My whole life has been taking it as it comes, and that philosophy has worked out pretty well. The Bucs needed to make salary cap cuts with so many high-profile players wanting to get paid. I never really looked at the moves. I was enjoying the moment and waiting to see what was next. I know Jon would have liked having me around. He might have said it was as a player, but it really would have been more of an assistant coach role. Coach Muir asked me about my plans as well.

**Muir:** "I remember it was the night of the Super Bowl, or the morning after, and we were sitting together. He wasn't sure what he was going to do. I talked very earnestly with him about becoming a coach because he had done such a great job with these young guys and I just watched him. He has natural teaching ability. The attention everyone gave to him was because he was an extremely accomplished player, and here he was able to articulate the techniques that helped him play so well. A lot of players aren't able to articulate to another player how to improve his play. I really thought he would be great at it, and he'd have a great career in coaching, but I think he entertained it...for about an hour or two."

The thing about coaching is that you have to *love* it. It's a whole different lifestyle. You're putting in crazy hours. Gruden would work in the office until like midnight and then be back at work by 4:00 AM. Some guys sleep in their office. Years later when I was a coaching intern with the New York Jets, then-head coach Eric Mangini used to video conference bedtime stories for his children. Jon *lives* football. He used to tell me that he didn't have any friends. The guys on the team were his only friends. I've thought about coaching off and on, but it was never really a passion for me.

After the championship the offseason was another cosmetic training period. I like to call it the "fat boy's" workout. I was taking care of my parents and waiting for another chance to play. Nothing transpired by training camp, but I stayed in decent shape. Then I got the call.

Bill Cowher wanted me to join the Steelers. Pittsburgh was off to a slow start and needed help on the line. It was clear the team lacked leadership, so he thought of me. Not only that, but he wanted me to start…immediately! His plan was that they'd fly me in Monday. I'd practice Wednesday and Thursday, travel Saturday, and play that Sunday.

I really wasn't sure if this was a good idea, but Coach Cowher was a salesman at heart. Plus, their director of player personnel was Kevin Colbert, who I knew from the Lions, and he wanted me, too. The Steelers ran a gap system, so my job would be to just shift left and shift right. It'd be easy to pick up. Heck, if I'd been in that type of system my entire career, I probably would have been an All-Pro 10 times!

By the time I got off the phone, Cowher had convinced me that I could do this. I went to sleep. The team set my flight for 6:00 AM, and

I was going to join the Steelers. At 3:00 AM I awoke and called my agent. Naturally, he was worried about why I was calling. I had tossed and turned and decided that I couldn't do it. My career was over.

A couple of years later, when the Steelers won the Super Bowl in Detroit, I saw Coach Cowher and apologized, and he was very gracious. He told me I was welcome to visit with his team any time. Even after the flirtation, I still kept playing in the back of my mind. I never even filed my retirement papers until four years later.

\* \* \*

I learned valuable lessons during my NFL career, especially with the Lions. If you're going to spend 18 years of your life doing one thing, you'd better learn some lessons during that time. I had a lot of ups and downs during my NFL career. There were times that I felt like I was on top of the world, and others when I wasn't sure how I was going to get to the next day. But each year, each team, each experience taught me something.

I would say the biggest lesson I learned in Detroit was resilience. The season before I was drafted, the Lions had won only four games. Straight up, they weren't a very good football team. Because they had such a high pick, I knew the situation wasn't good. It was an entire change in my environment. Remember, I grew up down South, and now was dropped in the Midwest, so there were a lot of changes for me personally while the team was trying to put pieces together. Here I was, coming off a season at Florida where we went 9–1–1 and were supposed to play for an SEC championship. We had a ton of good players and a lot of success. Now, I was arriving at the bottom.

The Lions tried to go about things the right way, drafting four offensive linemen. Building a team is like building a house. You've got to start with the foundation. That year, selecting Glover and me was the first step. But we knew the process wasn't going to be easy. There were going to be twists and turns, and hopefully we'd end up where we wanted to. The biggest accelerator, of course, was Barry Sanders. Once he came to town, we just took off. Still, it was a process.

With the Lions I learned how to hang in there, how to weather the ups and downs. If you look at it, it's kind of the way of the fanbase. I mean, it's been since the 1950s since the Lions won a title, but there are the fans, showing up every Sunday, even in an 0–16 year. They go to training camp each season, thinking this *might* be the season. My attitude was that if the fans are like that, I needed to be as well.

Looking back at my career, how it got started, the different places I got to visit, and winning the Super Bowl in my last game, as upset and hurt as I was in leaving Detroit, it gave me a chance to play in two Super Bowls. My philosophy is that everything happens for a reason, and you need to be flexible. It would have been easy to retire after my year in hell…I mean Cleveland. But I never would have gotten to the big game and never would have my Super Bowl ring.

Over the course of a career, or a life, you'll have lots of struggles and disappointments, when it feels like nothing will ever go your way. But if you don't persevere, you'll never know what's ahead. Probably the most talented teams I ever played on were in Detroit, but we weren't *complete* teams like the ones that went to the Super Bowls. It's not always about the end result, it's about putting yourself in the right position to have good things happen.

# Chapter 12

# Bennie and the Ball

During my time in Detroit, we had some pretty high-profile players, including Barry Sanders, Herman Moore, Chris Spielman, even myself. But two of the most productive guys were sometimes overlooked: Bennie Blades and Jerry Ball. How anyone could look past Jerry is beyond me. He had a huge personality and stood like a pit bull at 6'1" and 330 pounds. And if anyone forgot Bennie, well, they never played against him.

Jerry came to Detroit as a third-round pick in 1987 out of SMU just before the season where the Mustangs received the death penalty and lost their football team. My first reaction was: *What will this little cannonball be able to do?* That didn't last long, as his athletic ability was off the chain. This was a guy who was converted from the fullback position in high school. The only word I can use to describe his athleticism is awesome. Plus, he fit right into our culture because he was all about the team. I love that guy.

As tough as he was on the field—and he was one mean SOB— off of it, he was a teddy bear. He was nicknamed "the Governor" because he was the guy everyone would go to for answers to questions, guidance, or just as a sounding board. It's important to have a guy like that on your team or even in your business organization. We all have times where we need support or advice, and even your girlfriend or wife can't help. Jerry was that guy. When younger guys were trying to figure out how to play in the league, they'd go to the Governor. And old guys trying to figure out how to stay in the league also would go to the Governor. Having someone be able to fill that role is as important as having really good players. This was one thing that fit Jerry like a glove. He *loved* being that guy. Jerry was also on Wayne Fontes' players committee and really a true leader.

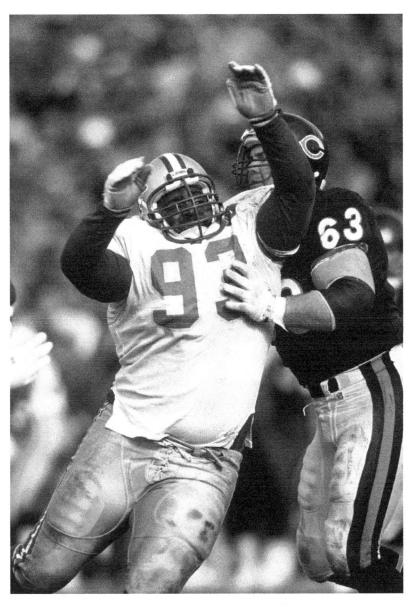

The Bears try to block defensive lineman Jerry Ball in 1991, something offensive linemen struggled to do.

Let's get one thing straight: Jerry was a great guy and leader, but he could really play, too. He went to three Pro Bowls and made one All-Pro team. People rightfully talk about how Barry revolutionized the running back position. The fact is, though, that there was only one Barry. I also think Jerry's impact is still being felt today, even though he played his last game in 1999.

Jerry would take on two or three guys and just make them irrelevant. It was like they weren't even in the game. That allowed the rest of the defense to make tackles. What was crazy was it wasn't like he was out there freelancing. This was all done within the scheme. Even now you see some linemen who are just lumps that try to tie up linemen. Sure, Jerry could do that, but he was so versatile that he could be like Warren Sapp and disrupt the whole offense with his penetration. You just couldn't run against him.

There was one time when we all learned this lesson, and one player learned it the hard way. When we're practicing there were some unwritten rules: don't hit Barry, don't touch the quarterback, and only go at about 50 percent effort. The game is so violent that the last thing any team needs is a guy getting hurt when it's *not* during a game. One day we had a young lineman (luckily for him, I don't remember his name) who was taking things a little too seriously. This young buck decided to cut block Jerry.

Big mistake.

The Governor wasn't being too politically correct when he stormed back to the huddle—the offensive huddle—and let us know, "You will *not* run another play." Now trash talking in practice was fairly common, so I don't know if we took that seriously enough. But I'll be damned if Jerry wasn't telling the truth. Five plays later Wayne had to pull him out of practice because we couldn't get another play off. He just destroyed that kid. The second the ball was snapped, the other Ball was in the backfield. Lesson learned.

One of the biggest disappointments to me is that people didn't really appreciate Jerry. Go ask guys like Spielman, and Chris will be the first to tell you that without Jerry he wouldn't have been as successful. When you see the money that a guy like Ndamukong Suh got from the Miami Dolphins, he should be sending Jerry a thank you note.

\* \* \*

When you played against the Lions, it was pretty simple: you didn't come across the middle because if you did, there was a good chance you were going to meet Bennie Blades.

When Bennie was at "the U," the University of Miami, he had a reputation as a big hitter, someone who just punished receivers coming across the middle. So we had a pretty good idea of what we were getting, and the man delivered. This was the hardest-hitting, no-holds barred safety I've ever been around.

Me coming from Miami, and Bennie from Fort Lauderdale, I knew what type of personality he had. He was brash, which was just what you'd expect from someone from "the U." Back then it was okay to have the attitude. Big-time football players from Florida were celebrities. Guys like Sapp, Bennie, and his brother Brian were hot stuff, and they knew it.

But that reckless style took a toll, and Bennie paid the price. He was always dealing with various ailments during his career, but there was no doubt he'd be on the field. That was the thing back then. Guys like Bennie, Jerry, Spielman, Mike Cofer, we knew they'd be out there and we'd always get everything they could give. We had a great group. We had fun and partied hard, but the bottom line is that we played hard.

I remember one time when Bennie got a new nickname, "the Question Mark." His body was so beat up from throwing it around that he actually started to look like a question mark. He was slumped at the top and then curved at the middle. We got some good mileage out of that one, though the man still didn't miss any action.

For guys like Jerry and Bennie, teams don't realize what they mean until they're gone and have left the team. With the Lions back then, unfortunately, we were all just dollar figures to them. Thank goodness it's different now. These days the team will pay guys who perform like Matt Stafford, Calvin Johnson, etc. But back then, this was not the case. Think about the guys we lost: Spielman, Ball, Blades, Kevin Glover, myself, etc. These are the guys that helped build a foundation for your team. There's no number you can put on that. We were all good players, but more than that, we were family. When you look at the success we had, there was someone busting their ass to make it happen, but the Lions of that era just didn't want to pay.

# Chapter 13
# Crazy Characters

Idefinitely played with some characters, but there was no one crazier than my man Bennie Blades. Now the first thing I have to say is that Bennie was a great player. I mean, there's a reason he was the No. 3 overall pick in the 1988 NFL Draft. He was a terrific safety. He went to "The U" (Miami) and let everyone know it.

Here's a story that sums up how crazy this guy was. A bunch of us were out one night at a…well, let's say a men's entertainment club. Bennie wasn't happy with the goings on inside the place and had a couple of words with one of the other customers. He then invited the guy outside.

We followed Bennie because we wanted to make sure he was safe. Well, Bennie goes to his truck, but he doesn't pull out a handgun or even a machine gun. He pulls out a bazooka! I had never even seen one of those in person. I mean, who has a bazooka sitting in their truck? He never had to use it, but Bennie had said he was going to end the dispute and he definitely did.

## Big Boy Bubba

As a rule us linemen are big, and we can put down some serious food. Yes, I am in that group for sure, but I like to think I've always been able to keep things relatively in control. For my boy, Bubba Paris, that wasn't always the case. Big Bubba could play. He won two Super Bowls with the San Francisco 49ers during their glory years. He came to the Lions for the 1991 season and he showed that not only was he big, but coordinated, too.

But I'll never forget one image of him. Bubba was lying flat on his back in bed. He had a plate of food on his chest, along with a 32 ounce can of Hawaiian Punch and he was literally eating the food right off of his chest. And it's not like he was lifting his head above his chest. I mean it was right off his chest. Somehow, though, he made it through his feast without even spilling a crumb.

On the field, Bennie Blades was a great safety; off the field, he was completely crazy. (AP Images)

## Pro Bowlin'

I was fortunate to be selected to the Pro Bowl seven straight times. It was a different game in those days—a better game for sure. It was such an honor to be voted into the game. Back then, the voting process was done by our peers, other players. As the years have gone on, it's become as much about the fan vote as anything else. Guys get picked because they have a big name—not based on their play.

Now half the guys out there seem to be replacements for other guys who don't want to play. Of course, the last few years, the NFL has moved the game, and players who are in the big game don't play in the Pro Bowl. I'm not saying that back in the day it was *all* business, but it was a serious deal. I might be having a cocktail with Buffalo Bills defensive end Bruce Smith, but in the back of my mind, I knew that we'd be facing off the next day. There was definitely a pride factor going on.

Having said that, there was still time for fun in Honolulu, especially if your name was Charles Haley, the Hall of Fame defensive end with the 49ers and Dallas Cowboys. As crazy as he was on the field, this dude was even crazier off of it. One night I learned that the hard way.

Our outing started right after practice at like 10:45 in the morning. As the evening progressed, I was getting ready to call it a night but not Charlie. He was still on the rampage, talking about where he wanted to go, where he wanted to hang out. This guy was hilarious. Here's one of the best football players in the world, and he'd walk up to people and tell them he was someone else. He'd jump in their conversations, drink their drinks, and it was one of the funniest things I've ever seen.

I later found out he got back to the hotel at about 3:00 AM. This was a good lesson learned. I couldn't keep up with the crazy guys like Charles. There are professionals, and there are professionals. People like Charles, or Lawrence Taylor, they were old school; they'd party all night and then be ready for practice the next day like nothing had happened.

# Chapter 14

# **Great Opponents**

When you play as long as I did, you play against a lot of great guys. It seemed like every week I'd be battling against Hall of Famers. Here are the toughest matchups I faced.

### Lawrence Taylor (New York Giants linebacker)

With L.T. it was more of a mental intimidation thing. I've seen those videos, *The NFL's Greatest Hits*, where Lawrence is telling everyone, "We gonna go out like crazed dogs!" I've seen him destroy tackles. I watch *Monday Night Football*. I saw him break Joe Theismann's leg. I've seen that guy destroy offensive tackles.

When I was being recruited by his agent, Ira Black, I got a chance to be around that dude, so I knew what I was getting ready to face. Without question the first time I was getting ready to face him was the longest week of my career. I was so nervous that whole week, but I actually did pretty well. I was proud of myself, though I got beat a few times. Before the game you go out there and warm up, and a friend of mine, who went to Florida and is a TV producer, told me that they had all these L.T. cameras. Keep in mind this was back in the '90s before TV sports became such a huge deal. He told me they had like six cameras just focused on L.T. to track everything he did on the field, on the sideline, wherever. This man had cameras just to follow his every move! So that meant that every play, I had a camera on me trying to stop him.

I faced L.T. three times during my career, and I matched up pretty well, but you had to be at the absolute top of your game to take on that man. That was your week of preparation, everything had to be perfect that week. He had one of the greatest motors ever. He would just come and come and come. The shocking thing was that he didn't talk a lot, at least not when I played against him.

### Richard Dent (Chicago Bears defensive end)

Oh yes, Richard "Dirty" Dent had that nickname in college at Tennessee State, and I could see why. The dude was smart with some great moves, but he seemed like the total opposite of L.T. because he's a talker. He wouldn't talk directly at you, but he'd talk to the sideline and coaches. He'd always talk to Wayne Fontes about what he was going to do, and I'm not talking about good stuff. He never did anything dirty to me, but this dude was crazy. He'd be trying to kill you for 60 minutes, but as soon as the whistle went off, he'd be like, "How's the wife and kids? How's the family?" It was just amazing how he could turn it on and off.

### Chris Doleman (Minnesota Vikings defensive end)

We came in together. He was drafted two picks ahead of me in 1985, so we kind of grew up together. We played in the same division (the NFC Central), so we played against each other twice a year. It was like having a sibling. This guy just blossomed into his body. He started as a linebacker but filled out and was able to play defensive end. He was just a great player. He was a guy you had to sit on the inside of because he had a lot of great moves. The thing that Chris used to like to do was just bull rush you. I'd be trying to force him to run the corner. But what Chris would do is he'd run the corner, plant his foot, and just come right into you. As a lineman you'd want to kick him to the outside, but he'd bull rush you and drive you back into the quarterback because you had no balance. He was great at that. Chris was a quiet guy, but he had help. John Randle talked enough for everyone on the Vikings line.

One of the best opponents I faced, Minnesota Vikings defensive end Chris Doleman, gets the best of me and brings down quarterback Rodney Peete during a 1993 contest. (AP Images)

### Bruce Smith (Buffalo Bills defensive end)

I came in with him, too. We were real close when we first came in together in the 1985 NFL Draft, but we grew apart. We met on the Walter Camp All-American team. I remember that in our first couple of years, we had Buffalo in the preseason, and he'd come and pick me and Kevin Glover up. He was a great player, the all-time sack leader. The thing about Bruce was that he was an athlete despite his bad knees. He could use his leverage with his dip move, where he'd lower his shoulder and lean into you. That's hard to deal with because he was 6'3", so it was difficult for tackles to get down to his level. He could also set you up really good. He'd almost do like Dent did, where he'd limp like he was hurt, then *BAM!*

Late in our careers, when I was on the New York Giants and he was on the Washington Redskins, someone did an article about the Geritol matchup. Even in that game, he'd be helping me. He'd be asking, "Why you backing up so far? Why you keep backpedaling?" It was weird. I've got huge respect for him and his 200 all-time sacks. He was a great guy and a great player.

### Derrick Thomas (Chiefs defensive end/linebacker)

D.T. and Seahawks linebacker Rufus Porter were the fastest guys I ever played against. It was like playing against a cat, that's how quick Thomas could change direction and come underneath. He'd stop on a dime. As a tackle, you're kicking to the outside and you can't stop with all of your weight. He was the only guy who could move like that. I remember when he set the record with seven sacks against Seattle because he was moving like that all game. Half the time the guy didn't even touch him. Derrick was like 250 pounds and could still run and move like a guy who was much lighter.

### The Mouths that Roared

As much as I talk these days, I was never really one to run my mouth on the field. I'm not sure why. But it was never something I ever got into. Some guys were legendary smack talkers, like L.T., but like I said, he was actually pretty quiet when we matched up.

That wasn't the case for John Randle of the Vikings.

To be effective at talking shit to the opponents, you need to come up with something creative. That's where John's after-hours preparation came in handy. He was infamous for doing his research and using it to his advantage. We were playing Minnesota one year at the Silverdome, and nothing was out of the ordinary. The two teams always had a fierce rivalry, and we were just playing typical NFC North football. Then came a TV timeout, and it was showtime for John.

He looked right at my teammate and fellow linemate Mike Compton and went to work. He barked, "Hey Mike! How's my wife (John knew her name) and my two daughters (of course, he knew their names too)." The next thing I knew, Mike blew a gasket! The rest of us were still in the huddle, and Mike is screaming, "I'm going to kill you, you son of a bitch!" We tried to calm him down, saying this was exactly what Randle was hoping for, but Mike was not listening. Eventually, we were able to restrain him, but that was one time when Kevin Glover and I just giggled to each other, and said, "Damn."

\* \* \*

In my year with the Tampa Bay Buccaneers, we had a really good running back named Michael Pittman. One day, we're playing the Cleveland Browns, and they had a safety by the name of Earl Little. Well, Earl had dated Michael's wife before they got married. We knew going into the game that Earl was going to let Pitt have it. And he didn't disappoint.

The festivities started in the second quarter. I can't even repeat what he had to say all game long to throw Michael off. He talked about having relations with Mrs. Pittman, things like that. Guys will say anything to get into your head—all in the name of getting a competitive advantage.

\* \* \*

Like I said, I wasn't a huge victim when it came to talking trash, but in this league, *no one* gets out of there unscathed. Probably the best anyone got me was Hall of Famer Randy White. It was my rookie year, the first time I played against the Dallas Cowboys, and it was already intimidating enough. The frickin' star on the side of their helmet looked so big! I was in awe. I mean, this was America's Team, and these were the guys I had always watched on TV.

We were in a television timeout (when it seems like a lot of this stuff happens), and all of the sudden without any provocation, Randy started cussing me out during the *entire* timeout. He talked about my mom, called me every type of MF'er you could think of. Nobody else is paying attention, and I just keep looking back at him, wondering, *Why is he picking on me instead of anyone else?* All I could think was, *Dude, this guy is crazy!* Luckily, he was on the inside of the defensive line, so I didn't have to tangle with him much, but that dude definitely intimidated me that game.

## The Games Within the Game

Whenever you're watching a football game, you know there's going to be tackles, touchdowns, and other exciting plays. Most of the time, you'll also see a fumble or two. I'm telling you the one place you do not want to be—under any circumstances—is at the bottom of the fumble pile. Don't get me wrong, it's really exciting. Defensive players talk about how sweet the hit was and how they don't even feel it. Offensive players are in a mad scramble trying to figure a way to get the ball back. No matter what, you *will* pay the price. Dudes will do anything and everything in that pig pile. They'll pull on your genitals, punch you in the stomach, poke your eyes; it doesn't matter. Anything they can twist, they will. And you almost never see any penalties get called.

Let's face it: football is a violent game. What's dangerous is that fans don't get to see a lot of the abuse. We were playing the Bears once, and I was matched up with William "the Refrigirator" Perry. The Fridge was only 6'2" but weighed in at an "official" weight of 335 pounds. He was a tough guy to move.

Well, I had a couple of nice cut blocks that left him on the ground. A cut block is basically falling on the guy's legs while he's engaged and can't escape. After the second cut, Fridge got up and very calmly said to me, "Do it again, and I've got something for you." Sure enough, a couple of plays later, I cut him again. This time he fell on me spread eagle. Perry's listed weight of 335 pounds wasn't doing the big boy justice. So he's lying on me with no urgency to get up. I thought he broke my ribs. I couldn't breathe! That was the last time I cut him that game.

Whether it's under the pile or not, guys will do anything and everything for an edge. One of the biggest examples in recent history has been the New England Patriots and "Deflategate." Truth be told, I think the NFL made a bigger deal out of it than they really needed to.

I get it when the skill position people say it's an advantage, and that is true. But the linemen still needed to block for Tom Brady; the defense still had to tackle. In other words all of the other things that have to be done without the ball, they still had to be done at a high level. I think the commissioner was just looking at things for more of the principle of it, the integrity of it. The competitive advantage warranted a suspension, but it's more because it was a kind of repeat offense after the Patriots got their hands caught in the cookie jar back in Spygate, so I think it stems more from that.

Guys used to scuff up the balls all the time. Some quarterbacks would let the kickers kick the balls around to make them feel worn. Now during my career, I never knew about PSI, but they'd pour rubbing alcohol on the balls to get the sheen off of them. So while I think there should have been some punishment for the Patriots, I wish the league would have just come out and said it was because of past transgressions.

# Chapter 15

# My All-Time Lineup

When you play 18 years and for five teams, you're around a lot of great players. Whether they were teammates or opponents, I've always appreciated watching the best. I get asked a ton of questions like *who was the best at this? Who was the best at that?* So I decided to put together a list. The rules for being on my dream team are simple. I was an offensive lineman, so you had to be an offensive player. The other qualifier is that you had to either play with me or against me.

### Head Coach

The biggest name during my career was Bill Parcells. He won two Super Bowls and went one other time. One thing he's most known around the league for is his coaching tree. With that being said, it shouldn't be a surprise that the head coach for my dream team is...Bill Belichick.

Is he Mr. Personality? No. Even when he does interviews, does he ever really say anything? No. But this guy is all football, all the time. When I was with the New York Giants, we spent a few days in camp with the New England Patriots, and it was beyond impressive to see how he handled things. There were 20 different things going on at any given moment, but he was on top of all of them. Every drill had a specific purpose. When I tweaked my leg one day, he was the first guy to come over.

I'm not sure what happened in Cleveland, where he failed, but he is one hell of a football coach.

### Quarterback

Growing up in South Florida, I've never hid the fact that I'm a dol-fan. So of course, my man was Dan Marino. I just loved watching this guy. In my opinion he gets a little overlooked because he didn't win a Super Bowl, but that's not fair. Everyone knew Dan didn't have a running game like other teams, and his defense was spotty. The easy part of the gameplan was figuring out Miami's offense. Dan would throw, and throw, and throw. But even when teams knew what he was going to do, he still did it and still won. He was awesome.

### Running Back

Seriously? You may have heard of this guy named Barry Sanders.

### Running Back

Here, I'm going with "Sweetness," Walter Payton. Like Barry, he wasn't a big guy, but he ran *hard*. It felt like every time we played them, he'd be good to break five or six tackles. And he wasn't one of those guys who would go looking for the sideline either. He liked the contact, craved it. As tough as he was on the field, he was soft-spoken off of it. Wow, was he great.

### Wide Receiver

Thank goodness I had a good career, or I would have been known as one of the guys drafted ahead of the GOAT, Jerry Rice, who was in the same 1985 draft and selected 16th overall. Sure, he had some talent, but this was a self-made player, who used to strengthen his hands by catching bricks. Some critics say he benefitted from the 49ers' West Coast Offense, but trust me, he would have dominated in any gameplan. If it was around him, he'd catch it…and likely take it to the house.

### Wide Receiver

I'm going with my old teammate, Herman Moore. He wasn't flashy, he wasn't fast, but he had the best hands I've ever seen. What a luxury for our quarterbacks—they could throw it anywhere around him, and Herm would make the grab. He was also a precise route runner, and that's how he got open. All receivers coming into the league should watch film of him playing. That's how you catch a football.

There is no doubt that Barry Sanders would be the running back on my all-time list of great players. (Courtesy Detroit Lions)

### Tight End

You've got to be tough to play tight end, and there weren't many guys tougher than Mark Bavaro. He just *looked* like a football player. He was a devastating blocker and a good receiver. He always had a great YAC (yards after catch). He won two Super Bowls with the New York Giants and played with the Philadelphia Eagles and Cleveland Browns, too. His biggest problem was what made him great; he played so hard that his body couldn't handle it. Guys today are just pass catchers, but this dude would put a helmet on guys as a terrific blocker. Injuries shortened his career, or he would absolutely be in the Hall of Fame.

### Right Tackle

Speaking of a career cut short, Erik Williams was one of the best tackles I'd ever seen. That Dallas offensive line was one of the best, and a big reason Emmitt Smith was able to put up a record 18,355 yards. But a lot of those Cowboys got into trouble off the field, and Williams got into a car accident. He played a few more years but was never the same. You can ask Michael Strahan about him. Erik had some incredible feet, but he never got the credit he deserved. His specialty was a cobra/snake move, then a head butt, and next thing you knew, you were off your game.

### Right Guard

Another Cowboys lineman, Hall of Famer Larry Allen, used to just dominate, plain and simple. He was so strong. He could bench press 600 pounds. But he would pull and create holes for Emmitt. Their line was just ridiculous with him, Williams, Nate Newton, Mark Stepnoski, and Mark Tuinei. They weren't choirboys, but they were among the best.

### Left Guard

On his way to a 19-year, Hall of Fame career, Bruce Matthews came out of USC as a strong player and he just got stronger and stronger. He excelled in small areas, and his brain was right there with his muscles. Perhaps the most impressive thing is that with his father, brothers and sons, the Matthews have had *six* players play in the NFL.

### Left Tackle

I went with two guys here because I can't possibly choose between them, and they're both in the Hall of Fame. You can't go wrong with Willie Roaf or Jonathan Ogden, but they did things differently. Jonathan was slightly ahead of Willie as a technician. He was 6'9" and never got caught out of position. He was so big that once he got his arms out, you just couldn't get around him. It was like he just swallowed you up.

Willie would sometimes let his weight blow up, and maybe that's part of the reason he was traded from the New Orleans Saints to the Kansas City Chiefs. No matter what his weight was, Willie never lost his foot speed. As big as he was, he'd get you out in space, and nobody could see around him. Jonathan was the better pass blocker; Willie was the better run protector.

### Center

Like I said with Marino, I'm a proud dol-fan. I loved watching Dwight Stephenson because that dude used to just dominate guys. I'm talking about destroying good players. His career was cut short by injuries, but he was incredible. He was so good that he was inducted into the Hall of Fame in 1998.

### Kicker

Let me start by saying that I love Eddie Murray and Jason Hanson. They made a ton of clutch field goals for the Lions, and they're both friends. But I worked out with Morten Anderson. This guy was incredible. He kept retiring, then coming back and he wasn't coming back to be average. He played for five teams (twice with the Atlanta Falcons) and made seven Pro Bowls. Mort put in the time to be great, and it worked. He'll get to the Hall of Fame soon.

# Chapter 16
# The Hall of Fame

I am always getting asked if Hall of Famer Barry Sanders was the best running back of all time. I also get questioned on why he retired. But then I also get asked a Hall of Fame question about myself—namely, will I ever get into the Pro Football Hall of Fame? The answer is, I don't know.

Let's be honest, getting into the Hall would be the ultimate achievement. To think that someone could come from my beginnings and be enshrined with the best ever to play the game is mind-blowing. There's so much that goes into the voting: how did the player get along with the media? How many guys from the same position will get voted in? Every year my friends get all fired up when I don't get voted in and send texts, call, etc. And believe me, I appreciate the support. But I don't really get caught up in the emotion. Every year, when the class gets announced, I do pause for a second. Truthfully, it stings a bit, but then I let it go. We'll see what happens.

**Barry Sanders (former Lions running back):** "I think you can make a strong case for Lomas being in the Hall of Fame. I think of the All-Pro years, the guys he competed against, the Hall of Famers he went up against, and he played exceptionally well. I'd have to go back to that era to see who got in at his position, but I think he stacks up favorably with all of them. There's no question about it. The only reason he doesn't get it is because defensive linemen get more attention than offensive linemen, but yeah, he definitely deserves to be in."

**Wayne Fontes (former Lions head coach):** "If they looked at every film and looked at it critically, they'd know that Lomas was a way above average football player. Lomas should be in the

Hall, but sometimes a guy gets overlooked early in his career if he wasn't a Super Bowl tackle, but Lomas should be in the Hall."

**Rob Rubick (former Lions tight end):** "He should be in the Hall of Fame. I mean, you play 18 years in this league, wow! I see other tackles that are in there and I'm thinking that I don't think I'd trade them for Lomas. Lomas didn't look as imposing. Remember, he was lean, 270 to 280 pounds for a lot of his career. When he walks into the room, the room doesn't disappear. He looks like a really big tight end. He was able to play with that body for 18 years!"

**Chris Spielman (former Lions linebacker):** "I do think of him as a Hall of Famer. Obviously, I'm a little biased, but he was tremendous, big guy. He was physical, tough, and he played consistently, played injured, and was reliable. Offensive lineman is one of the hardest positions to gauge performance. I was very close with Eric Andolsek and watched a lot of film with the linemen. I always really enjoyed watching Lomas. You'd see things like his great balance, footwork, and that tenacity. Yes, I certainly think he was Hall of Fame caliber."

I look at the Hall the same way as my career. I never expected to be in the NFL, let alone play for 18 years. Everything just comes for a reason. If it's meant to be, I will be honored to be voted in. And it would be great if it happens next year, but it would be even bigger in, say, 2020. I say that because I didn't win a Super Bowl until my last season. That gave it more meaning than if it was in my first couple of years.

Honestly, I'm fine either way. The good news is that even if I don't get in, I will always be a Super Bowl champion. Having said that, I do think I belong, without a doubt. If you look at the great running backs, guys like Emmitt Smith, Eric Dickerson, and John Riggins—they all had to have some help. Without a great line, they'd never accomplish what they did. My hope is that the voters look at Barry's career and realize that there *was* someone who helped him.

In addition to Barry, I've played with five other Hall of Famers, so I know what it takes to make the Hall of Fame. Here's my breakdown of those great players.

### Aeneas Williams (Arizona Cardinals)

This was my guy and the best cornerback I ever played with. Aeneas was a deeply religious guy, but I call him the quiet assassin. A lot of people think that if you're a man of faith, you just keep your mouth shut and play, not 'Nee. The difference was that when he talked trash, it was mostly bible verses! When I came to Arizona, Coach Tobin wanted me to help lead the team. Because Aeneas was so great, it made my job easier. He led the defense, and I just had to worry about the offense. It might be difficult to follow such a nice guy, but he was the ultimate lockdown player.

### Michael Strahan (New York Giants)

We used to kiddingly call each other "BBM" for big bitter man. His locker was near mine, and it was a pretty simple routine: the media would circulate the room, getting what they needed, and then when Michael came out of the shower, *everyone* flocked over to him. We had lots of great conversations on the team planes. He *loved* cars. At one point he had like 12 of them. He was physically a lot stronger than people realize. By the time I got to New York, Mike was in his fourth year and was really starting to develop as a leader. People ask me all the time if I thought he'd be such a big television star. Well, kind of. Of course, I knew he was made for TV, but nobody could have imagined he'd own the industry like he does. It's about the right guy, at the right place, with the right agent. He walked right off the stage of the Super Bowl title to a media star. Everyone thought Tiki Barber was going to be the big media star, but there's no eclipsing Michael.

### Derrick Brooks (Tampa Bay Buccaneers)

I love this guy, even if he went to Florida State. All of us who are from Florida have such pride in our hometowns and our alma maters. Things like being on the all-time Florida team are a big deal for us. DB was a tremendous linebacker. I've always thought he'd be a great ambassador for the league. He's humble but can take (and give) a joke. A man with strong beliefs, but not overly religious, he is such a good man that he started a charter school in Tampa. I'm proud to call him a friend.

### Warren Sapp (Buccaneers)

Yes, Warren has made as much news off the field as he did on it. He's had his issues, no doubt. But I love my homeboy, always have. He's a good dude overall. I've known him for years, but we really bonded on a different level when I went to Tampa. As with DB going to FSU, Warren and I were on opposite sides—with him going to Miami and me to Florida, but we always understood each other. I knew he was wild, that he had that side to him, but make no mistake, he was a great football player. With some people, trouble just kind of follows them around. Warren is that guy, whether it's marital problems or issues with drugs. He has a good heart. When I was working at ESPN, I used to call him all the time, looking for information about a certain player. Even now, anything he needs, I'm there for him.

\* \* \*

And I know he wasn't a teammate or a Detroit Lion, but I want to quickly mention one other Hall of Famer—Reggie White—because he was the most dominant, but polite guy I ever played against. He was a great guy…off the field. It's such a shame that he passed away so young. He was just 43 years old. On the field, though, he was a monster, nearly impossible to block. There's a reason he had 198 sacks. You'd figure a man of the cloth, the man nicknamed "The Minister of Defense," would be the last person to talk trash during a game. At least that's what I thought. I was wrong.

Reggie was the only guy I've ever seen who combined religion and violence in the manner he did. We'd be lining up, and you'd hear guys grunting, saying stuff about your family. Nothing was out of bounds. But this man would pray for you *before* he kicked your ass! I can still hear the sound of his voice, "John 3:15," then *WHAP*! He'd knock you over. Like I said, Reg was a great guy, so he'd help you off the ground. Then he'd drop another bible verse.

# Chapter 17

# Growing Up with the Browns

I grew up in Liberty City, Florida, which is in Northern Miami. It is also one of the state's poorest and crime-ridden cities. It was a pretty rough neck of the woods in the 1960s, but we didn't have many problems there. The Brown house was blue collar; we didn't always get what we wanted, but we did always get what we *needed*. My dad, Lomas, was a hardworking man of few words. He really just kept his head down and did his job. My mom, Annie, worked in the medical supply field. I have an older brother, Jeffrey, who lived with my grandmother in Georgia, while my other brother, Gary, and my sister, Valerie, and I all lived with my parents.

My parents were a great example of how opposites attract. Dad was ultra-private and didn't express his feelings. Although nobody would ever mistake me for quiet, I looked at him as a role model. I really think that the way he went about his business kept me out of trouble because I never had to hang with a big group or anything. Dad had a couple of friends but was private, and I followed suit. We listened to my dad. If he told you to do something, he'd just put the fear into you. He didn't really scream or yell, but it was just his voice. It taught us to respect our elders.

Mom, on the other hand, was also someone I looked up to but in a different way. The Lomas Brown you see today resembles my momma's personality much more than my dad's.

She was the affectionate one with the kisses, telling us how she loved us all the time. As reserved as Dad was, Mom was 180 degrees the other way. It's funny how times change. My mom worked full time, took care of three active kids and a husband, ran the household, and never said a peep about it. In the era I grew up in, it's not like women had a choice. My parents were out of the house first thing every morning, and we had to make sure we left at the same time. There were no sick days or just hanging out at home. We were up and ready.

Here I am at 11 years old—well before I would grow into one of the NFL's best line-men. (Courtesy Lomas Brown)

Dad was a construction worker and became a steward for the union. His main responsibilities were to make sure members were up to date on their dues, and if they weren't, he'd send them home without work. It was not a popular job, but he was really the perfect man for it. He never asked for special treatment and never gave it.

Our big break was when I turned five. My parents scraped enough together to move us out of our apartment in Liberty City and out to Brownsville. Our house was nothing extravagant: three bedrooms, one bathroom, kitchen, and living room. We also had that room that I think everyone had growing up, the one with furniture wrapped in plastic. You could look, but you'd better not touch!

Brownsville was such an improvement for us. Times were different back then, but everyone knew each other, and we were always helping each other out. I don't remember much trouble in Liberty City, but it was the projects, and who knows how I would have turned out had we stayed there.

We had a pretty simple life in the "Brown Sub." Our house was modest, but it was *ours*. I know it was a big deal, especially for my dad. You had to be able to read through him to appreciate him. He was proud. He just didn't feel the need to show or talk about it. We were movin' on up just like the Jeffersons.

I was a pretty good kid, never getting into much trouble. But there *was* a three-day stretch back in either fifth or sixth grade that made sure I stayed that way. I've always been someone that just likes being around people. Well, during one period at Lorah Park Elementary, I was spouting off, being the class clown. It was nothing too serious, but my teacher was not impressed. After repeated warnings she told me she'd call my house and talk to my parents.

Keep in mind, these were the days before cell phones, and we didn't even have an answering machine. But that night I was feeling a little skittish, so I did what any other kid would do: I took the phone off the hook all night. The next day, I was feeling pretty smug, having outsmarted my teacher. She told me again that she'd be calling the house, and this time I wasn't worried about it.

Big mistake.

Mom took the call and listened to everything her not-so-little angel was up to in school, disrupting class, talking back to the teachers, etc. Then she told Dad. I'll give my father credit: he told me he was going to make me sorry and he lived up to his word. Remember, he was a construction worker, so he had the big mitt-like hands, and they were hard. He'd come home from work and then beat my ass with a belt for three straight days! Those construction hands? One would hold me by the ankles, and the other would just whip me time and time again.

Let's just say I never had a problem in school again.

Lesson learned.

The only other real discipline issue I had with Dad was when I was around 16. You don't realize this until you're a parent, but raising teenagers can be your biggest challenge in life. You're 16, growing some hair on your chest. I like to say you're smelling yourself. Well, let's just say that I was sniffing myself some Lomas at this point and thought I was the big man around town. One day, my father told me not to touch his car, which was in the driveway. So you know that the young superstar, with license in hand, had to take the car. Now I only went around the block. There was no accident or anything like that.

Until I got back home.

As I pulled into the driveway, there was Mr. Brown, and he was not happy. I never even got out of the car. Dad reached through the driver's-side window and *clocked* me right in the chest! I never crossed my dad again.

My parents never had any trouble with my sister, Valerie. Don't get me wrong, I love her to death, but that girl had a halo around her. She never got in trouble ever. She was the youngest and the only girl. The rule was that you couldn't put your hands on her. And even when she did something wrong in our house, she was Teflon—nothing ever stuck. Me and my brother couldn't say anything to her. We couldn't look at her cross-eyed without getting busted. Like I said, I love her, but she was the golden child, and she used it to her advantage.

I don't necessarily think of myself this way, but she always said I was kind of quiet and shy. I played in the band and didn't talk that much. My brother, Gary, was a different story. He was a year younger than me, and, while we were close, we couldn't be more different in our approaches. When Dad told us to do something, I'd do it; he wouldn't. Gary was in and out of jail from the time he was 14. He's just crazy. He got kicked out of so high school so many times that he had to go to an alternative school, which was actually the same one that Pro Football Hall of Famer Derrick Thomas graduated from.

He got into drugs and didn't straighten out until he was in his late 30s. Gary once told me that he actually liked being in jail more than his freedom. I think he felt that behind bars he knew he wouldn't get in any more trouble. It did seem like he did better in jail probably because of the discipline he had to deal with. Having Gary as a brother has not been easy on any of us. He cost me anguish and money. At one point I moved him up to Michigan to stay with me. I figured the closer eye I could keep on him, the better off he'd be. He'd borrow my car, pile up a bunch of tickets, and never tell me. Then, all of a sudden, I'd get these notices in the mail about how much money I owed.

During the Miami riots, everyone was looting the local stores. Gary and I would see people going down the streets with new TVs and all kinds of high-end electronics. He convinced me that we should go get ours. Our parents had stressed to us *not* to leave our home. At first I resisted, but Gary wore me down, so we decided to go loot for ourselves. Where did the Brown brothers decide to steal from? BF Goodrich. So while our neighbors were getting new stereos, we were on the hunt for tires!

As was the case most of the time when I tried to do wrong, this episode didn't go too well, either. The plant was full of looters. Everyone was stealing hubcaps, tires, and everything else. Things were so frantic in the area that the police stopped going into stores. Instead, they'd just drive up and down the streets ringing their sirens. Everyone would flee when we heard the sirens. While running away, I didn't see the steel doors, which slashed my leg.

When we returned home, my mother looked at the gashes on my leg, and it was obvious that I needed stitches. But there was so much violence going on, that we'd never get into a hospital. I still have the scars today. My parents were so mad that I wasn't allowed to go anywhere for a couple of months. I'd go to school, then back home. I wasn't even allowed to go to band practice. At the time it was a very serious cut, but as the years have gone on, I can look back and laugh at it. And whenever I think about doing something stupid, I can just look down for my own personal reminder.

You'd think growing up in the South at that time period, we'd have to deal with a lot of racism, but that wasn't really the case. It was nothing like South Beach is today. Back then, Miami was where the snowbirds from the North would come. In my opinion there were three factors in how Miami of the 1970s and '80s turned into the Miami of today.

One of the big changes came when President Jimmy Carter provided safe harbor for refugees, who had fled seeking U.S. citizenship. They realized the future of their homeland was bleak and risked their lives looking for the American Dream. That was the start of "Tent City." You could drive down I-95 and see tents upon tents full of people. Many of these were good, hardworking people, but there were also criminals and mental patients.

One of the upshots of all of this was really just logistics. I grew up on 55th Street. Down on 36th Street is where many refugees started to settle. White folks were already in Coral Gables. That pushed blacks out into different parts of the city. So not only did African Americans need to move, but when word got out that the new immigrants were getting stipends to live there, the you-know-what hit the fan.

The second big change in Miami is something we hear about even today, which is police shootings. The big one in this case involved an insurance salesman by the name of Arthur McDuffie. Mr. McDuffie was stopped in 1979 doing 80 mph on his motorcycle. Further complicating matters was that he had several citations already and was driving with a suspended license. Four police officers chased him through the Miami neighborhoods—first by car, then on foot, before finally apprehending him. According to the police, Mr. McDuffie resisted arrest, and a struggle ensued. McDuffie suffered a fractured skull and would die a few days later in the hospital.

Three of the officers were charged with felonies, including manipulating evidence (the other was given immunity for testimony). As was the case years later with the Rodney King case in Los Angeles, and similar cases in Ferguson, Missouri, and New York, the police officers were acquitted, which led to total chaos.

In the span of three days, 18 people were killed, more than 350 injured, and property destruction was more than $100 million. Aside from the violence, angry people raided their own neighborhood, looting from stores, which, of course, did more damage to themselves than anyone else. In my opinion the third reason for the shift in Miami is simple—drugs. Miami has never been the same.

### Learning the Game

I never played organized sports until I got older. Nope, I was on course to become the world's largest trombone player! In the seventh grade, I decided to give football a shot. We had Optimus football, which is similar to Pop Warner. They organized kids and teams by weight. Of course, I was too big and had to shed a few pounds.

On the first day, we were doing conditioning, conditioning, and more conditioning. Kids were throwing up all over the place. To wrap up practice, the coaches had us run three laps around the field. I got through the second lap...and kept on running out the gate. Gary went back the next day, but I was gone. Football was not for me.

So I decided to try out for basketball. To say that my coordination was lacking would be an insult to coordination. We had this one game, and I was on a fast break and went up for a dunk...only to have the ball get stuck between the rim and the backboard. Some of the girls in my class just tore me up, saying, "You're big, but you're sorry!" They told me I sucked and couldn't play. I skipped some classes for two days because I was so embarrassed.

Playing in the band, though, that was pretty cool. I played the trombone in the seventh, eighth, and ninth grades. I made it all the way to second chair. That was no easy feat, especially for a kid with braces. Think about how hard it is to keep on blowing, while my lips were bleeding. My parents supported me in whatever activity I was doing. But there were times when it was tough love, especially from Dad.

One day I was walking home with my buddy, and this guy came up to me with a knife, and told me to give him my trombone. I looked around, and my friend was gone, I was on my own. The trombone was like $200 to $300. But this dude had a knife! I wasn't messing around.

So I came home and told my dad. He was hot! Forget the fact that his boy was traumatized, he wanted the instrument back! So he drove me back to where the guy stopped me because he wanted me to get it back. I didn't want any part of that. I was glad that the guy was long gone.

As great as it was when we moved to Brownsville, there was one negative. When it came time for my high school years, our school zone was redistricted. I was supposed to attend either Miami Northwestern, Miami Jackson, or Miami Edison. Instead, I had to go to Miami Springs. This meant waking up at 5:00 AM and leaving the house at 5:50, so I could catch the city bus. That took me to a stop where I caught another city bus. That one took me to yet another one. At that point I could either take a third bus or just walk the rest of the way to school.

Looking back, yeah, it was a pain to get to school every day, but it did make me get used to following a schedule.

On my first day of high school, I was registering for my classes, when I heard a voice. It was my principal, Mr. Alex Bromir, asking if I'd signed up for varsity sports. Of course, the answer was no. The only thing I played was the trombone. That wasn't going to fly for the principal. He grabbed me by the arm without saying anything and signed me up for varsity sports. He saw a 6'3", 190-pound freshman, and the next thing you know I was a football player.

What struck me with Mr. Bromir was that I didn't want to let him down. That's just the way I've always been. I hate disappointing people. Whether it was my parents or my teammates, I want to carry my load. As bad as my brief basketball career went, the start of football was just as awful. The coach put me on the offensive line, but I needed help. And I mean big-time help. Forget not knowing the plays and that I had no footwork. I didn't even know how to put my pads on. My sister told this story that really captures how my first stint in football went. "I don't think he really liked the sport," Valerie said. "When we were growing up, we'd play, and I'd be the only girl out there with all of the boys. I think I was tougher than he was! He was scared out there. He didn't know what to do—like a fish out of water. He had some natural skill, but it was buried deep inside. I think if it wasn't for the football coach and Dad making him play, I don't think he ever would have played football."

But then came the turning point in my football career, really in my entire life. And it came from a driver's education teacher. Frank Battaglia was another one of the basketball coaches as well. Mr. Battaglia came to me one day, and asked me a simple question. "Lomas, do you want to be good?"

I answered yes, and my life was never the same. He laid out a gameplan for success. It started with the right attitude. We worked six days a week every week. Now remember, he had coached basketball, not football, but he taught me how hoops could help me in football with footwork. I don't know how he did it, but this guy knew *everything*.

He was like Professor Higgins in *My Fair Lady* with me playing the role of Eliza Doolittle. Mr. B was like a second father to me. He taught me about society, about life. I had only eaten my mother's soul food, and then he introduced me to Italian food. He even showed me how to set a table and which fork to use for salad. In a nutshell he made me realize there was a whole world out there beyond the Brownsville Sub. It always seems like people come into your life and it isn't apparent why. Frank Battaglia and Rick Garcia helped me by working with me for hours.

## The Biggest Loss of All

In 2004—two years after I retired—I suffered the biggest loss of my life. Both of my parents died just six weeks apart. Even now, years later, I'm still grieving. My father had been in poor health since even before my career started. But to his credit, Dad didn't give in. He couldn't really work but was able to get around pretty well. Because of the blood thinners he took, we knew he couldn't travel to Detroit in September, but he was able to do the things he wanted to.

I remembered how proud we were when we moved into the Brown Sub. But once my pro career started, I was able to move my parents out of there into Rolling Oaks and let them build their dream house. Mom loved cooking and going to restaurants, and I'm happy they were able to do that. Mom was only 67 years old when she passed, and that, combined with the loss of my father, left me incredibly bitter. It just isn't fair that she was so young, but cancer knows no age limits.

My dad wasn't an emotional guy, but I miss the little things, like watching sports. He didn't use many words, but if we got talking about sports, it was awesome. Dad was a great example of the adage: it's not what you say and that actions speak louder than words.

I miss being able to go to both of my parents for advice. Think about it, your life is full of major decisions—where to work, who to marry, all kinds of things. It doesn't matter if you're a million dollar athlete or not, you are going to have a journey. You never stop learning, and that's what your parents are there for. They always have your best interest at heart. No matter what, they are always going to be your parents.

I miss seeing (and smelling) my mother working in the kitchen. My older kids were able to have a relationship with their grandparents. The younger three are too young to really have had that bond. It hurts me that they didn't really know my parents and never had the chance to soak in their wisdom. I guess that's part of the reason why you have siblings. I've always stayed close with my two brothers, but my go-to person is my sister Valerie. She really helped me during the grieving process.

**Valerie (my sister)**: "He took it pretty hard because he wasn't here [in Florida] physically and wasn't able to see them in their last days. He was always close to my parents, especially our mom. It really took him a while to get over it. We'd call and talk to each other. That's how I got through it, and him as well...We've always stayed in touch, we were always the closest two."

You've got to have someone in your life, and Val has always been that person. I was the first one she called to break the news about the passings of Mom and Dad. I never realized how great it is to have a sister. Men, we think one way, but you need to be able to bounce it off a woman to get that female perspective. Just like my parents, she's my biggest advocate. She only cares about what's best for me; she never wants anything else.

Especially when you're a pro athlete, you never really know why people want to be next to you. A lot of them have ulterior motives. It's the brutally honest truth. Being an offensive lineman, none of us had a "posse," but I've seen it too many times with guys like Barry Sanders, Warren Sapp, Keyshawn Johnson, and others. They'd get these hanger-ons, people I like to call "crumb snatchers." It's like they're behind you, looking for any crumbs. Now don't get me wrong, there's nothing wrong with it, if they're bringing something to the table. I mean, there's enough for everyone to eat. But still, they're making their living off of you.

It's not like that with family members and it's never been that way with Jeffrey and Val. Now that I'm out of the limelight, the income's not the same. I don't see any crumb snatchers in my circle. Would I like to make millions of dollars again? Sure, but these days, I know who my real friends are.

## My "Spine"

That's how I describe my wife, Wendy. She's my backbone. People talk about how opposites attract, and that's Wendy and me. I'm much more open than she is—probably to a fault. I let people in fast and don't take the cautious route. Not my Wendy; it's like in *Meet the Parents*. You have to prove yourself to get in her circle of trust. And she's not shy about expressing her opinion. She's more of an observer, taking it all in. If there's anything that she feels uncomfortable with, you can be sure Wendy will let me know about it.

This is my second marriage, and it's just been great. The first time around, I was still playing football and didn't really have the opportunity to be as big a part of my kids' lives as I'd have liked. Wendy has given me a second chance at being a dad. She's 10 years younger than me, and that has honestly kept me feeling younger.

I've also been blessed to have a second chance at being a husband and I know that I'm better at it this time around. I've changed a lot, and that's due to Wendy. She gets me out and doing things. This girl is a real whippersnapper. She'll say, "Hey, me and the kids want to go to Mexico," and I'll be like, "We'll see." Three weeks later, she's booked and ready, having already bought the tickets. I do my best to keep up with her—whether it's in Mexico, Costa Rica, or Spain. I just love Wendy to death; it's impossible to see myself with anyone else.

## My AAA Girls

I have three kids from my first marriage: Antoinette (30 years old), Ashley (28), and Adrienne (26). We have a great relationship now, but it wasn't always that way.

My AAA squad was around 12 to 14 years old when their mom and I got divorced. For a long time, there was just a lot of bitterness. Divorce isn't easy on anyone, especially teenage girls. They blamed me, and I knew it. On top of that, it was around the time I signed with the Arizona Cardinals. I was far away, and we didn't really communicate much.

Eventually, my ex-wife and I sat down and said if we're going to raise productive kids, we had to mend our relationship, be civil to each other. Once the girls saw that we were able to mend our relationship, that was a huge turning point. Now that they have their own kids, they're seeing firsthand that life isn't always fair or easy. It truly puts a lot of things into perspective. We have a really good relationship. I love being a grandfather, and we get together on a pretty regular basis.

## The Next Generation

Wendy and I have two children together: 16-year-old Lomas III (we call him Trey), and Jayla, who's 14. My goodness, teenagers are a lot of work! It's been great, but I'll tell you that it's been challenging like nothing else. I've been reminded that they aren't always going to do what you want them to. Kids don't see the wall they're running into, but we parents do. We want to protect them, but they don't understand. That's one reason I miss my parents so much. If I listened to some of the things they told me, it would have been so much easier. But that's the way of life. It's all about the experiences you're supposed to have.

What's cool is that Trey and Jayla are at the ages where we can sort of see what they're going to become in life, but I can still mold them. The older kids, you try to help, but they're already set in their ways. They have their personalities already developed. You try and advise and help them as much as you can. They'll always need guidance. You're always going to be a parent. They'll always be your kids.

Trey loves sports, including football, but I think he might like lacrosse better. He goes to different football camps every summer. One thing I decided is that I'm not going to push him. I try not to coach him in football. The last thing I want to do is criticize him and make him feel like he has to be me. Jayla might be the best athlete of all my kids. This girl is like lightening. She's so fast and she has a motor; she's a pistol on the basketball court and in track. There's no question that she hates losing more than the rest of the clan.

# Chapter 18

# Choosing a College

For a guy who never even played organized sports until high school, and despite my awful start, I really hit my football stride by my junior year, and colleges were starting to take notice. Of course, my size—6'3" and around 230 pounds—didn't hurt either. Football has, in many ways, been a parallel for my life. I didn't chase after the game; it came to me. Remember, I tried out for different sports, but it wasn't until high school that with a gentle arm twist from my principal, I became a football player. For college it was the same deal. It's not like I was out looking for a scholarship, but by my junior year, the schools starting coming to me.

Miami Springs was a hotbed for recruiting. We had players like Freddie Miles (an All-American running back who signed with the University of Miami), Anthony Frederick, Carl Sheffield, and John Cruz. These guys were idols for the rest of us. Unfortunately, they didn't pan out at the next level. I think the difference between my path and theirs came down to one word—family. My parents essentially created a shelter for me. We knew the difference between right and wrong, and except for a couple of minor bumps in the road, I was able to stay on the straight and narrow. These guys were huge talents, but they weren't able to stay on track.

It was from guys like this that I learned about the not-so-fun side of recruiting. I remember seeing Anthony running down the hall, trying to escape recruiters from Nebraska. The same thing happened with Carl. He used to say, "Don't tell them where I am!"

We had a good team my senior year, and I don't say this boastfully, but I was really the main target for recruiters. There were some other guys that got attention, guys like Ed McDuffie, Brent Goins, and Craig Jay but I was the main target. When I got to school, they were there. When I got out of class, they were there. It felt like every move I made was being watched.

When I was graduating, football in the state of Florida was dramatically different than it is now. There were still great high school players in the state, but the "big three" schools hadn't really developed. Florida State was just bursting onto the scene. Bobby Bowden arrived in Tallahassee in 1976. By the '79 season, the Seminoles were in the Top 10. FSU, though, wasn't a realistic option for me.

My dad wasn't a man of many words, but I usually got his message loud and clear. He grew up in Tallahassee back in the 1920s, and racism was rampant. As Dad told me, he used to run moonshine just like in the movies. He'd have to drive with the car lights off at night, so he wouldn't get caught. Furthermore, Tallahassee was a big home of the Ku Klux Klan. Because of his experiences there, I was not going to Florida State.

Another school that was on the rise was the University of Miami. The Hurricanes were just a year or two behind FSU. New coach Howard Schnellenberger came from the NFL, where he was the offensive coordinator for the undefeated Miami Dolphins team in 1972 and head coach with the Baltimore Colts.

One of the biggest reasons behind the rise of "The U" was that Coach Schnellenberger started recruiting in Liberty City. U of M was known as the mafia down there. He knew there were a ton of poor high school athletes there, and they'd do nearly anything for a few bucks.

The pressure from Miami and Coach Schnellenberger was nonstop. They had coaches waiting for me outside of class and at every game. When my dad had a heart attack while I was in high school, Coach Schnell showed up at the hospital. By the time Dad was home, Coach Schnell had him hook, line, and sinker. He sat there with my parents and said, "In three years, we're going to win the national championship. I want your son. He's going to help me."

Back in those days, it was commonplace for schools to set up their athletes in sham jobs. Miami did that when they were trying to get me to sign. I'd go to my landscaping "job" for about three hours a day and get paid like $150. Miami was a hidden jewel. It was a private institution, so they could get away with stuff without anyone finding out.

Even with a treasure trove of athletes in the area, kids weren't going to "The U" until Coach Schnellenberger arrived. Things had started to improve when future Bills Hall of Famer Jim Kelly was in Coral Gables, but it was the coach who made the big difference. And Schnellenberger was true to his word, too. Three years after sitting in my house, the Hurricanes indeed were national champions.

To most people the recruiting process probably sounds like the coolest thing ever. Everyone is telling you that you're the greatest thing since sliced bread, how you are the missing piece to a championship. They *at minimum* are offering to pay for your education, books, and living accommodations. In many other cases, they're offering more (we'll get into that in a minute).

But I'm here to tell you that recruiting ain't all it's cracked up to be.

The other school that came after me the hardest was probably Oklahoma University. Coach Barry Switzer would do anything to get what he wanted. The Sooners were the kings of the wild, wild, west. Coach Switzer not only told me that within six months I'd have enough money to buy a car, but he even offered to put my girlfriend (and first wife) on full scholarship. Switzer was one of the best at digging deep into Miami to find players. One of them was Buster Rhymes, a defensive back from Northwestern High, who played a couple of years in the NFL and would be the source of the nickname for the hip-hop star. Another was Troy Smith. He was a great offensive lineman back in the day. He never panned out in Norman for a couple of reasons. First, when you're talking about college ball, Oklahoma is no joke. That was the big time. Second, I think Troy probably got a little homesick. Out there, especially in the early '80s, there wasn't much around. I remember that I could literally see the campus from 20 miles away. It was that flat.

Of course, it would have been nice to have a car and the other perks, but something didn't feel right about Oklahoma, so the Sooners were out. I also went on a visit to the University of Pittsburgh, and believe it or not, the Panthers were actually my top choice. Where Oklahoma and some other schools were offering stuff like cash and cars, I did get one illegal benefit from Pittsburgh. It was so cold, and me being a southern boy, I didn't have a winter jacket. So one of the assistant coaches gave me his. That's probably not what some recruits were looking for, but it kept me warm.

The Panthers were in their heyday. They'd won the 1976 national championship with Heisman winner Tony Dorsett, who was followed by future Super Bowl champion Jimbo Covert.

Pitt encased the lockers of each of its All-American players. Looking at Mark May's locker, it was the first time I'd ever seen someone with size 16 shoes. Believe it or not, that was actually an inspiration. Bill Fralic was also there during my visit. I was totally infatuated with the area. It was like a city within a city, a concrete jungle, if you will. There was no question in my mind, I was going to become a Panther.

The other visit I took was to Ohio State University. Coach Earl Bruce had started tapping into Miami with recruiting, landing future New York Giants offensive lineman William Roberts, among others. I was supposed to visit OSU's archenemy, the University of Michigan, but there was a pretty big problem. The temperature was nine degrees during my day in Columbus. That was cold enough. I wasn't visiting Ann Arbor. For years, my future teammate with the

Lions, Bubba Paris, gave me grief about not at least checking out the Wolverines. Big Bubba had been scheduled to be my host.

So Pitt was it, or so I thought. That's where fate intertwined. During the last game of my senior year in high school, my dad suffered a heart attack at work. We were fortunate that my uncle was working with him, and he saved his life by getting Dad to the hospital. They didn't tell me what had happened until after the game. Dad survived, but he was physically diminished for the rest of his life and was unable to work full time again. That shifted my thought process, and I knew I had to stay home for college.

That opened the door for the University of Florida. The Gators, like Miami and FSU, had a relatively new coach, Charley Pell. In his first year in 1979, Coach Pell went 0–10–1, but the next year the Gators were 8–4 and ranked 19th in the country. As is often the case in recruiting, I didn't deal with the head coach often. It usually falls more on the assistants. My main contact was Mike Brown, who I met when I was 15 years old. He was a southern white guy, but we just connected. When we'd go out to dinner, people would just look at us like the biggest odd couple ever. Mike is a good man, and he and I are still very good friends. He made sure once I got to Gainesville that my parents never missed a home game. The school put them in hotels, made sure they had tickets, etc. I heard that some of the bigger-name players got stuff like houses or cars, but I was happy with what I got.

Dad remembered that Gainesville was not a happy place for the black community at one point and didn't want me to deal with that. But this was 1980, and things were different. Still, being Dad, he never really expressed his feelings, but if you look at my scholarship letter today, you'll see that it has two signatures—mine and my mother's. Dad never signed it. It was hard for me to understand how on the happiest day of my life that my father wasn't really a part of it.

I mentioned that when my parents left the house in the morning, so did all the kids, no matter what. This even included the summer, when we still had to attend school. The benefit of this was that I had finished all of my high school work by the middle of my senior year. This allowed me to sign with the University of Florida in late January and head out to Gainesville.

Charley Pell was one of the most intense coaches I ever played for. Pell played at Alabama under Bear Bryant, and it was clear that the apple didn't fall far from the tree. Coach was all about the mind games. In his office his desk was always raised a couple of inches, so he could look down on visitors. Bryant used the same trick. Since I had dealt more with Coach Brown during recruiting, I don't think I actually ever spoke to Coach Pell until practice started.

Pell was a hard man. He was tough but fair. Like the Bear, he'd watch practice from his tower on the sideline, the better to see everything from, but also the easier to intimidate from. I remember one time that Coach didn't like something I did, and he called me over to the foot of the tower. He just lit me up, saying that I was practicing like a dog. I had never heard that before. The fact that Charley didn't take any crap was exactly like my father. I think that's why we always got along. As much as players say they want some freedom, I think most of them want discipline. I was definitely in that camp.

Future Super Bowl-winning coach Mike Shanahan was our offensive coordinator through 1983. Dwight Adams coached the linebackers. He was intense, but funny. His instruction for just about any situation was the same—"Git 'er done!"

Luckily, being a lineman, I was Coach Pell's kind of player. He wanted hard-nosed guys, who just did their job. No flair, no style. If you did that, you had no problems. His best attribute was that he knew *everything* that was going on. That's why he used the tower. The players would feel bad for the assistant coaches because they just got crushed.

Coach Pell, though, had a big problem. He was squarely in the crosshairs of the NCAA, mostly stemming from his days at Clemson. As we've seen before and since, when the NCAA has a target on your back, it's almost impossible to escape. During the investigation, the NCAA called me in for a meeting. Before going in there, I called Coach Pell to ask what he wanted me to say. He told me just to tell the truth—stuff about my family getting free tickets, about me selling my tickets for huge profits, etc. The good news for me was that all of that stuff was pretty minor. They were not like cash payouts. In the big scheme of things, my "transgressions" were just about being negligent.

The NCAA did come pretty hard after Mike Brown, as he knew everything about the inner workings at UF. With the NCAA, they know the answers before even asking the questions.

The ax finally fell on Coach Pell after three games of my senior year, and Galen Hall, our offensive coordinator/quarterbacks coach, took over. Talk about night and day, Hall was 180 degrees from his predecessor.

For an interim coach, I don't think anyone could have walked into a better situation. We were loaded. On our roster we had future first-round NFL draft picks Neal Anderson, Lorenzo Hampton, John L. Williams, and Ricky Nattiel, along with some guy on the line named Lomas. Our quarterback was a red-hot freshman named Kerwin ("Country") Bell.

While in college at Florida, I block future NFL Hall of Famer Kevin Greene during a 1984 SEC contest, in which we defeated Auburn 24–3.

We lost our first game to eventual champion Miami, when the Hurricanes scored two touchdowns in the last 41 seconds. We tied LSU the next week and took off. Nobody ever got within eight points of us the rest of the way. That made us the first team in Gators history to go 9–1–1. Our offensive line was known as the "Great Wall of Florida."

We clinched the school's first SEC championship with a tougher-than-expected 25–17 win at Kentucky. It was so cool to fly back to Gainesville and see Gator Nation waiting for us. We did two flyovers at the stadium, so both sides of the plane could see. We wrapped things up with a win at Florida State and awaited our fate. Remember, this was *way* before college football had a playoff and even before the

BCS. Teams finished out their schedules and had to wait for bids to play in whatever bowl. The SEC champion always went to the Sugar Bowl in New Orleans, but the SEC champion wasn't usually facing NCAA sanctions. LSU ended up going to the game, and lost to Nebraska 28–10. We should have been there.

## Prepping for the NFL

Just like watching older kids in high school helped prepare me for recruiting, the great players we had at the University of Florida gave me a taste of what the NFL was like. The best teacher was Wilber Marshall.

Wilber was a linebacker from Titusville, Florida, who was a year ahead of me. He ended up being a huge inspiration for me and my best friend, Ricky Williams. During my time as a Gator, I was really just living life, playing my game, focusing on the next opponent. Wilber taught us about the business of football.

This guy liked his money. He *always* had cash in his pocket and never less than $1,500. I remember one time, he whipped out $1,000 and spread it on the bed. He came across a $5 bill and threw it away and said, "What's that doing here?"

Wilber was the 11th pick in the 1984 draft and was taken by the Chicago Bears. Soon after, he showed up at our dorm room and showed Ricky and I his signing bonus—for $1 million! I had never seen that many zeroes! Now I knew guys who had been drafted. The year before, our running back, James Jones, was taken in the first round (by the Lions) and he was making some good money, too, but Wilber was more of a showboater—not in a bad way. He was just more playful than anything else. When he got that bonus, he made sure he used it. Wilber bought two twin Mercedes coupes—one in red and one in black.

After my junior season, I was the 83$^{rd}$ ranked prospect. After seeing Wilber and his success, things changed. That's when I put a photo of a new BMW 735 on the wall. That was my goal. I was going to work so hard to get drafted high enough to get me one of those.

As the draft approached, I had no idea where I was going to be playing. By this point, I had a grade for the first half of round one, but that was all we knew. The Cleveland Browns (originally the seventh pick), Philadelphia Eagles (ninth), and Green Bay Packers (14$^{th}$) showed the most interest, but I never spoke to anyone specific from those teams. I let my agent Peter Johnson handle all of that. Peter worked with IMG, which was and is a huge agency. I probably should have stayed with them, but their other clients were Herschel Walker, Jack Nicklaus, and Arnold Palmer. I felt like a tadpole in a huge pond.

One team that never contacted me was the Detroit Lions. Neither Peter or myself ever heard from them.

Today, there's no mystery when it comes to the NFL Scouting Combine. Hundreds of the country's top college football players show up in Indianapolis to run through drills, take tests, and meet with teams. You can watch the whole thing live on NFL Network. ESPN is there every day, and even the casual fan can come up with opinions on who his team should draft and who looks good.

Back when I graduated, things were different.

On the plus side, we got a trip to Arizona State University in Tempe. Unlike these days, a lot of potentially high picks—like the No. 1 pick in the 1985 NFL Draft Bruce Smith—didn't even show up and for good reason. I felt like we were a herd of cattle. We'd be standing in lines wearing nothing but shorts. Teams would poke us, prod us, measure, and weigh us for their records. We took the

Wonderlic test, which gives teams an idea of our intelligence and ability to learn. We also did interviews and ran drills like the vertical jump, 40-yard dash, and shuttle run.

I'm not sure if I was invited to the NFL draft in New York City. Regardless, I didn't go. Smith was the top pick, going to the Buffalo Bills, Bill Fralic (who was still mad at me for not going to Pitt) went second to the Atlanta Falcons, and Ray Childress was the third pick to the Houston Oilers.

I knew I'd get chosen early, but I didn't know where. The Eagles and Browns had showed the most interest, but I knew anything could happen. And it did. Once the Minnesota Vikings took Chris Doleman (a future Hall of Famer), I got the phone call that would change my life: "Lomas, this is Daryl Rogers from the Detroit Lions. If Minnesota takes Doleman, we're going to draft you." That was the entire discussion.

At No. 5 the Indianapolis Colts picked linebacker Duane Bickett from USC. The phone rang again. It was Coach Rogers. "Congratulations, you've been chosen by the Detroit Lions." I was speechless, and my new head coach picked up on it.

"Aren't you excited?" He asked.

"Uh, yeah," I responded.

It was more shock than anything else. Sure I *was* excited about getting picked, especially so high, but of all the teams I thought about, the Lions were not one of them.

**Bill Muir (Lions offensive line coach)***:* "It was [Daryl Rogers'] first year. Wayne Fontes was the defensive coordinator, and we were going to make the change from the 4-3 defense to the 3-4. So the focus on the draft was we needed a dominant linebacker. We were sixth, and that was the year that Duane Bickett of USC and Chris Doleman of Pittsburgh came out."

**Bill Keenist (Lions assistant public relations director)**: "My first official day with the Lions was the day we drafted Lomas. I was working for the Debartolo family in Pittsburgh with the Penguins primarily. I was wrapping things up and flew in for the draft...We had the sixth pick, and the expectation was that we were going to draft one of two linebackers, Duane Bickett or Chris Doleman. Because of projections of the teams ahead of us, we were pretty sure we would get one of those linebackers."

**Muir**: "All of the draft gurus had it all figured out that there was no way in the world that either Bickett or Doelman wouldn't be available to us. So everyone went into the draft room, and we just knew that one of the guys were going to be the pick and we were going to be happy no matter which one it was."

**Keenist**: "I think Minnesota traded down, and that tipped the cart a little bit, and they ended up taking Chris Doleman, and the Colts ended up taking Duane Bickett."

**Muir**: "A silence hit the room. Everyone in the room was stunned. The clock's ticking, and we're like, *What are we going to do? What are we going to do?* There's no Plan B. Daryl Rogers immediately spoke up, went up to the draft board, and took Lomas' name off the board. He said, 'I coached him at the Blue-Gray game, and he's a hell of a football player, a better person than a player. We can't miss with this pick.'"

**Keenist**: "We had actually scouted Lomas, but I'm not sure we had any interaction with him at all. So it was almost, 'Well, he's the best player on the board.' There was no hesitancy to select him, but going into the draft that day, there was no expectation that he was going to be a Detroit Lion."

**Rob Rubick (Lions tight end)**: "A couple of years prior to Lomas, we drafted James Jones from Florida. James ended up being one of the best picks the Lions had in the past 10 years. He was actually able to fill in when Billy Sims got hurt. The resume with Florida stood well with us, taking Lomas in the first round."

Fans follow their teams a whole lot more closely than athletes do. Growing up, I was all about the Dolphins. Remember, in those days, there was nothing else in Miami. (The Heat didn't become a franchise until 1989.) I really knew nothing about the Lions, other than they play every year on Thanksgiving. And as far as my Detroit knowledge? Well, being a southern boy, the only time I'd really ever been up north was when my family took a road trip to visit relatives in New Jersey. I knew four things about Detroit:

1. That's where they built cars.
2. It's the murder capital of the U.S.
3. There's a high population of African Americans.
4. It's cold!

**Keenist**: "My NFL experience prior to that was with the Washington Redskins and 'the Hogs,' and Joe Bugel, who became a close friend, was the offensive line coach on the team. From that experience I learned that the most important unit on a football team was the offensive line. They were the engine. Of course with the Redskins, they had the most popular offensive line, if not the best in all of football at the time, so I was predisposed to have a high regard for offensive linemen. I just remember loving Lomas from Day One. There was just something about him, and it remains to this day. He's on my Mount Rushmore of all-time Lions that I've worked with without question."

**Muir**: "He had a great athletic ability. For a big man—and he was a *big* man—his combination of size and athleticism gave him a distinct advantage at a position where athleticism is probably the primary commodity."

**Rubick**: "It didn't take long when you saw Lomas. For as big as he was, he had tremendous feet. A lot of rookies come in and in the pass protection, that's where they struggle, especially when we got tackles from the Midwest, and it was run-blocking first in the '80s, then pass-blocking second. But for Lomas, I think he was a better pass blocker initially because of his athleticism. He's the only guy who could get beat in pass blocking and recover. The guys you watch today, they get beat, and it's right to the quarterback. Lomas—it looked like he was half-beat around the edge, but he could gather himself and get a piece of the guy running by the quarterback. That's what made him so good and last for so long."

# Chapter 19
# **The Media**

I don't think anyone was surprised when I decided to take a shot at working in the media. During my playing career, I always tried to be available and, even for an offensive lineman, I got a good amount of exposure.

**Barry Sanders (former Lions running back):** "I didn't necessarily see it coming. I know he knew a lot about the game and has a great personality. He's very likable. I just didn't know he would pursue that particular path. When you're around him, you see the man that he is and you take that many years of football, playing at the level that he did, playing against the players he did, and there's a lot there. He has a lot to give. So while I didn't see it coming, I'm not surprised."

In 2004 I had a tryout with ESPN. They teamed me up with former Pro Bowl cornerback Ray Buchanan. Sometimes things just work, and that's what happened with us. We connected right away, and "RayLo" was born. We spent four years together, working on *Cold Pizza*, which eventually became *First Take*, and we had a blast. If you think about it, I left the very best and most profitable league—the NFL—for the very best and most profitable media company—the Worldwide Leader. Who gets that chance?

*Cold Pizza* was based in New York and it was such a terrific experience. Getting to see all the behind-the-scenes stuff really gave me an understanding and appreciation for how everyone needs to pull together for the show to be successful. It was pretty similar to football in that regard. Being part of the team, that's how I've always been. A lot of that came from my parents and my upbringing.

When you're in a family, you always look out for each other through thick and thin. Now, you're going to bicker, you're going to fight. Hell, my sister sued me over money, and look how close we are. We didn't talk for a while, but you're going to get over it. That's family.

If you've got that family atmosphere, you can criticize someone. It's never easy, but you can do it. I'm a guy that responds to a coach. When a coach curses at me, that kills me. I can't do that. You can chastise me, but that's how I need to be coached. People take criticism differently. If you foster that family atmosphere, they know it's from a position of love, a position of wanting to help them. That's the kind of atmosphere I like to work in. When I was on *Cold Pizza* (and then *First Take*), Jay Crawford would go back to New York after the show, and me and Dana Jacobson—or Rob Parker, Derrick Brooks, Ray, whoever was in town—we'd go out and eat all the time. You get to learn about the person outside of work. I saw how it worked in the locker room. If you can take 53 testosterone-driven males and their egos, then you could apply that to anything in work. You see how close we are now. That's the main reason I watch ESPN now—to see my friends, Jay Crawford, Jay Harris, and all the rest. If Dana ever needs something, I'm always quick to do it. When she comes to Michigan, we try to hang out. We're all there for each other—for life. I became very close to the producers and talent like Jay Harris and Linda Cohn. Another friend is John Anderson, who was in Arizona at the same time as me, and used to fly on the plane with us. Jay Crawford covered me during my year with the Tampa Bay Buccaneers. And there was my Michigan girl, Dana.

**Dana Jacobson (former ESPN co-worker):** "My first Lomas Brown meeting is one I'll never forget, and he claims he has not. I was working as an assignment desk editor in Detroit. He was a star with the Lions. The World Cup had a Detroit venue. Lomas was an ambassador of some sort, while I was there with a reporter trying to learn how to report so I could start my TV career. I was introduced to Lomas by the reporter, and this big teddy bear of a man said the kindest hello. There's no way this was Lions offensive lineman Lomas Brown, but it was. He was like, 'Dana, you have to try the octopus.' There was some food there, octopus being one dish, and he wanted me to try it. It was awful, but Lomas said try it, so I did. He just had that type of effect.

Fast-forward more like 10 years later...or a little more, and in walks Lomas Brown to work on *Cold Pizza*. The teddy bear of a man that I remembered engulfed me in a hug, knowing I was a Lions fan. He swore he remembered our meeting (after I disclosed a few details). I have no idea if he really does, but it didn't matter. I could tell he was such a gentle giant, a genuinely good soul. He wanted me to know he cared enough to remember. Just hearing him say 'D'—he always called me 'D'—brought a smile to my face."

These people really helped teach me how to be on camera, how to present myself. Because I was an O-lineman, I was by nature pretty anonymous on a national level. ESPN gave me the platform to talk to millions and millions of people. It kept my name out there, which made me familiar to the younger generation. Even today, I can't tell you how many more people know me from TV than from my playing days. If you're out of sight in this world, you're out of mind.

I was really struck by the team attitude, the camaraderie that we all had. I try to bring that into any situation that I come into. To be a successful team, you've got to know your teammates. It's true in football and it's true in any other business. At ESPN we'd go out to eat and just hang out. Jay would be talking about his hometown Cleveland Browns, and me and Dana, we'd talk Lions, Tigers, anything Michigan. They knew I was committed to getting better and being a good teammate.

**Jay Crawford (ESPN anchor)**: "He always came in prepared and he was always willing to talk about whatever. He would come in, and oftentimes the segments would be hashed out in pre-show discussions. And he would never say, 'No, I don't want to talk about that.' Or that 'I don't have a great depth of knowledge on that topic, so I don't want to go there.' He had an opinion on all of it and he knew the current personnel. He stayed up on it, he had an opinion, and he was willing to share it. He was always nothing but prepared."

**Jacobson**: "He worked hard at ESPN. He could be so funny, putting on a Santa hat and giving out Christmas gifts to teams in need or he could break down game film. He didn't get enough credit for the latter because he was never trying to be controversial. Lo always told it how he saw it, was always honest with his opinions. Even now, years later, he's always there if I need him. And every time he says 'D,' I still smile.

"I loved watching Barry Sanders light up around him. At the Super Bowl in Detroit we had the whole *Cold Pizza* crew, and Barry came on the show. He's so quiet or was then. I was trying to make him feel comfortable just talking about growing up a Lions fan, blah, blah, blah. The moment Lomas walked up, the big fella made the little fella—I think that's what they called each other—smile. Barry was grinning ear to ear, and his stories just took on vivaciousness in talking about Lomas. Here were two guys who battled together, who had hopes together and watched many of those hopes dashed. They called each other 'Big Fella' and 'Little Fella.' It seemed like they'd do anything for each other, for the good of the team. It was just full-out loyalty. That's the thing—to know Lomas is to love Lomas. He was a fierce football player but again a teddy bear of a man."

In addition to Dana, another Michigan hookup was Rob Parker. Rob's not afraid to say what's on his mind, even if it ruffles some feathers. But he's a good guy, and I like that he's always straight with me.

**Rob Parker (former ESPN co-worker)**: "At ESPN if there was a crowd in the studio, it meant Lomas was chopping it up with behind-the-scenes people there. They were around Lomas. And as someone who has known Lomas since I first arrived in Detroit in 1993, I understand it. The term 'great guy' is grossly overused. Here with Lomas Brown, it fits perfectly...There's no one more gentle and kind. It doesn't really fit when you talk about a 6'4", 282-pound lineman, but Lomas was a human hug station. Not just at home, but everywhere. People can't help but to gravitate to Lomas. And I got to see it up close and personal.

"When we worked together at ESPN, we often were on the same travel schedule. So I saw him often. Walking through Detroit Metro Airport with Lomas was like walking with the mayor of the city. People couldn't help but come up to Lomas for a picture, a handshake, and hugs...And the scene played out over and over. That's what told me it was something special...Many of these people saw Lomas many times. Yet, they couldn't resist pressing flesh with the gentle giant."

Even as *Cold Pizza* turned into *First Take*, I always got along well with those guys, too. I had been on *Quite Frankly* with Stephen A. Smith, but I didn't have any connection with Skip Bayless. They quickly became friends. We were really a family, not just co-workers.

**Jacobson**: "I really enjoyed spending time with Lomas away from work. He'd be in a few days early in either New York City or Connecticut, and we'd grab dinner or drinks (although he'd usually just have an Arnold Palmer while the rest of us had a cocktail). He was just part of the family...He was one of the early adds to *Cold Pizza*, as we re-branded in 2005. We all were fighting to make the show work. We felt like we were on an island with just each other to rely on as a show unit.

"We had an early show trio to Vegas, did the show there for a week. I know what happens in Vegas stays in Vegas, but I think this part is okay to share. I'm not much of a gambler. I feel like if I'm going to take a chance with money, I should go buy clothes instead. At least this way, I have something tangible. I'll play a little blackjack but nothing major. Anyway, the last night, folks were at the craps table, and Lomas gave me a nice handful of chips to gamble with, an amount I'd never normally risk—and at craps no less! He just wanted me to have fun with the rest of them. If memory serves, I won a lot quickly then lost it all quickly because that is craps. But man, I had a blast! Next day at the airport, we had breakfast together and all we talked about was how much fun we had—not the money I lost, which was his money. He's got a huge heart and an infectious laugh, and I always felt like he'd do anything for me, that he had my back. I definitely have his."

It really was like a football season. I'd go there one to two times a week from September throughout the Super Bowl and then start over again the next year. It was important that we had that locker room setting. I wouldn't try to take over as being the leader; that's not how you do it. Instead, you learn about your teammates. You break bread with them. Soon, they'll realize that you care about them, and you'll gain their confidence. That's the lesson that Scott Mitchell never learned with us.

# Chapter 20

# Stafford, Megatron, and the Modern Day Lions

Unfortunately, losing is a part of sports. Even more unfortunately, it's been a major part of Lions history. Of course, the bottom fell out in 2008 when we went 0–16. It was the first and only time a team has done that.

The poor guy who was on the sideline that year was one of my former coaches, Rod Marinelli. Rod is a good man, and it made watching them struggle even more difficult. As an alumnus, you feel kind of helpless. You want to help, but there's nothing you can do. That's how I felt during the entire Matt Millen era.

When I see the successful teams around the NFL, it makes it even more difficult. They have stability, they make the right moves, and, as a result, they win games. That's what I want to see here. The fans and alumni in Detroit deserve that.

As a player there really is nothing worse than losing. It's like a contagious disease. Once it starts, it can be hard to put the brakes on. As the losses mount, you start to lose your confidence, and that's just *on* the field. The bad thing about losing is that it continues *off* the field, too. Food doesn't taste as good. You have a short fuse at home. It's like you're in a constant search, trying to find the answer. The natural feeling is to start second-guessing everything, but you really need to stay away from that. Like the saying goes: don't get too high over winning or too low over losing. Not everyone is cut out to be a professional athlete. That's one reason why there's so many divorces among players. They can't handle the stress and take it out on their families.

When things start going badly on the field, you look at the guys next to you—your teammates. There's so much on the line that it's pretty easy to see if a guy isn't pulling his weight. Some guys don't remember that playing this game is a privilege. Careers aren't guaranteed, and it doesn't last that long. I always tried to educate those guys instead of just casting them aside. My philosophy about the guys who are the problem? Well, they won't be around for long. They'll just weed themselves out. I don't want to be associated with those guys.

When the Lions went 0–16, people would always ask me if that was the worst team I'd ever seen. Well, there are only two teams that went a whole season without winning a game, and the Lions were the only one to do it over a 16-game schedule. So statistically, you'd have to say yes. But it's not that simple.

I remember playing for the expansion Cleveland Browns back in 1999. And to be honest, we stunk. But even that year, we won two games. The first was on a Hail Mary in New Orleans. The second came on a one-point win in Pittsburgh. My point is that all teams get a break at *some* point. The winless Lions may have been the exception to the rule.

Even though the modern day Lions have been a little bit up and down, it does seem like they've escaped the ineptitude of the Matt Millen era. There have been ups and downs, but at least they've been entertaining. Here are my thoughts on some noteworthy Lions of the past few years.

## Calvin Johnson

When Calvin was coming out of Georgia Tech, I remember the so-called experts talking about this huge talent as one of the greatest receivers of all time. Naturally, I was skeptical. I'm not anymore. This guy is the real goods. First, he's a genetic freak. People talk about LeBron James as the greatest athlete in sports, but I'll take C.J. He's 6'4", about 240 pounds, and runs like a 4.4 40-yard dash. He reminds me a great deal of Barry Sanders, and that's not something I throw around lightly. Calvin just comes in and does his business. He hands the ball to the ref after he scores. There's no showboating. He's very respectful to myself and other former players. Aside from Herman Moore, Calvin has the best hands of anyone I've ever seen.

Look at his numbers, and he's ahead of Jerry Rice in some catego-ries. Now don't get me wrong, Jerry is still the GOAT, but the league features more passing now, and Megatron is taking advantage of it. He's lived up to the hype, and that wasn't easy.

## Calvin's Early Retirement

In the summer of 1999, on the eve of training camp, Barry Sanders stunned the Lions by walking away from the NFL. Though it wasn't as big a surprise to those who knew B best, it was still a blow that in many ways Detroit never recovered from. In March of 2016, his-tory repeated itself when Calvin Johnson decided his body had gone through enough and retired after just nine years. Again, people were shocked, but you know what? Maybe we shouldn't have been. Barry and Calvin are very much alike. They are two once-in-a-generation players who cared about more than just numbers.

As you know, B was about 1,500 yards from becoming the game's all-time leading rusher. Shoot, that was an average season for him. Calvin is the best receiver in Lions history; there's no debate about that, but he only cared about the team, not his personal stats. When it comes to the best hands, I'll still take Herman Moore, but Megatron was the full package. Anyhow, neither Barry nor Calvin was a showy player. They'd do spectacular things on the football field, but you never saw those guys doing fancy end zone dances or putting themselves above the team. They were both dedicated to their craft. Another similarity is they played most of their careers before getting married.

Unfortunately, neither guy got to experience a Super Bowl; Barry only played in six playoff games, and Calvin only played in two. It's painful that Megatron's postseason career consisted of a three-point loss and four-point one. What made it worse was that both guys knew the team wasn't going to be winning big any time soon.

Each guy took a pounding but answered the bell every week. Barry was healthy and productive. He had rushed for more than 2,000 yards two years previous to his retirement. Calvin's yards per game had dropped for a couple of years, but he was still one of the top receivers in the league. He had started to really get nicked up with ankle problems, which as a receiver is tough to overcome.

Just like when B retired, some fans just didn't understand Calvin's decision. But this is a tough game, and if you've been pounded game after game for year after year, it takes a toll. Both guys seem to be totally at peace with their decision. And just like back in 1999, the Lions will find another guy to play the position. Though like in '99, there's no replacing a guy who's an all-time franchise great.

## Matthew Stafford

Of all the quarterbacks I've seen come and go through Detroit, Matt may have the most talent. This guy has serious ability. He's not as accurate as some, but he definitely has the velocity. But for whatever reason, it hasn't all come together. The biggest thing I *don't* see from Matt is the ability to rally his team. It's not really about being rah-rah during the game.

That's just what the public sees. I'm talking about getting guys together during the offseason, taking them out to dinner, just hanging together. During the season it means a Thursday night of buffalo wings with your linemen, calling team meetings. The quarterback needs to be the leader, kind of like the father figure of the group.

People talk a lot about how we used to have rookies get us donuts and breakfast on Fridays. The point wasn't some type of hazing or anything like that. We wanted to make sure the young guys were disciplined, and it kind of forces everyone to come together and break bread. The locker room is our sanctuary, and we can talk about problems or what's going on. I always looked at it like this: if I don't really know the guy next to me, how can I count on him to do his job and cover my back? That's what I think Matt has to do more of. And I know that there is a lot on Matthew's plate. I respect that he is stepping up and taking the challenge of leading this organization. Since he is the most visible, a lot of the responsibility of the organization falls on his shoulders, and Matthew hasn't shied away from that. Because of that, I would have loved to block for him. The one thing I know about Matthew is that he is tough, and toughness is one of the most important qualities in being a good football player.

Matthew Stafford readies to throw during an overtime victory against the Chicago Bears in 2015. (AP Images)

## Ndamukong Suh

I always found Ndamukong to be a really respectful guy. It was always, "Yes, sir" or "No, sir." He also has a great family, and I probably dealt with his sister more than him. There's no question in my mind that Suh could be the most dominating defensive player in the NFL because of his size, strength, and the way he plays. This cat plays with anger. He is old school, which is the biggest compliment I can give him. He reminds me of guys like Randy White. He's just plain nasty.

It's not easy for him with the Miami Dolphins because he's so good. I had a coach once tell me that if you make the Pro Bowl, things will never be the same. Everyone's going to look to make their name against you. Suh is awesome, and he's a Pro Bowler, but he's also the poster child for being a bad boy. He should get rid of his number 90 and just put a bull's-eye on his back.

He's been whistled and suspended for late hits and dirty plays. To be honest I don't have a problem with any of it if it was in the context of the play. We used to do all of the same things, but it was *during the play*. He's done this stuff after the play, and that's not the time to try and get even. If he could contain it to during play, everything would be fine.

## Head Coaches

Coach Jim Schwartz took over a team that was 0–16 and had them in the playoffs three years later. Obviously, he did some good things. I don't really have an opinion on him. Schwartz never gave us a chance to know him. I met him maybe five times in five years. It was never more than, "Hey Lomas, how you doing? You were a great player." I heard that he was a pretty good guy the first couple of years but not as much later on.

The Lions seem to have found their man in Jim Caldwell. I haven't been around him a lot, but I like what he stands for. This is a man of integrity. He doesn't say a lot, but when he does, it resonates. Where Coach Schwartz was pretty outspoken, Coach Caldwell seems to mean what he says and say what he means. He's kind of a father figure, which is great. I'd play for a guy like that any day.

## 2015 Lions

As far as the 2015 Lions. Wow, you look at the talent on that team, and it just doesn't make sense. Sure, Suh and Nick Fairley and Dominic Raiola all left, but you're still talking about a team with Stafford, Megatron, and a bunch of really good players. I still like Caldwell. Hey, they were 11–5 the year before and nearly beat the Dallas Cowboys in the playoffs. Did Caldwell and his other coaches get dumb all of a sudden? Last I checked, the coaches don't throw passes, make tackles, or kick field goals. This collapse, just like any other, is on the players. Do coaches have some blame? Sure, but it's the players who play.

Mrs. Ford desperately wants to win, but she's obviously not as patient as her late husband was. She and the rest of the family don't want to be associated with losing or records of futility. It's been that way long enough, and she's going to do everything she can to change it. I say: good for her. It's about time.

I've mentioned that over the past few years the Lions have done a better job of incorporating former players, but there's still a long way to go. When I see a team like the 2015 Lions—one that made the playoffs the year before but couldn't get out of its own way the next season—it makes me wonder why the organization doesn't reach out for help. Did the coaching staff get dumb overnight? Of course not, the players might just need to hear from a different voice for a period of time.

It's one thing to have us show up to sign autographs or even speak at schools, but why don't they call us in as consultants? I spent some time talking to offensive tackle Riley Reiff last year, and he explained the troubles he was having with speed rushers. I asked if he curled his toes inside his shoes prior to the snap. It's an old trick I learned that helps you explode off the line. Or the way you point your feet, which helps you do the same thing.

I'm not looking to become a full-time coach, but when you have guys living in the area—guys like myself, like Barry Sanders, Herman Moore—why wouldn't you lean on them? I mean, do you think Barry could help Ameer Abdullah with ball security? Could Herman work with the guys running routes? It's really a win-win situation. The team gets the knowledge of guys who played the game at a high level. They also build up goodwill in the community by reaching back to the past. We'd make a few bucks, and it's a way to help us with insurance.

Chapter 21

# The Future of the Lions and the NFL

One of the hottest topics in the NFL these days is concussions. The simple fact is that if you play this game long enough, you will likely have some type of head injury. I've been fortunate that most of my injuries were things like a separated shoulder, a sprain here, broken bone there. But what about my head? You hear the horror stories about ex-players suffering from dementia or Alzheimer's disease.

**Mike Utley (former Lions lineman)**: "I am the same as I was before the accident, the same as before I got crippled. There's only one injury that can make you change who you are, and that's a closed-head injury. If you allow someone to make you afraid, that's your fault. If you allow someone to allow you to be addicted to something, that's your fault. Be responsible. I chose to play this game."

That is classic Mike, holding himself accountable and not looking back. I've tried to take the same approach. The fact is, though, that a closed-head injury *can* change who you are. The recent studies of deceased players' brains keep on showing chronic traumatic encephalopathy or CTE. When you suffer injuries to other parts of your body, doctors can usually help. You see guys limping and in wheelchairs. Well, at least they are getting treatment to try and help. With your head, there's really not much. In fact they can't even diagnose CTE until you're dead. And as we know, the brain affects everything.

This is one reason I'm so proud of the work my old quarterback, Eric Hipple, is doing. Hip is the outreach coordinator of the University of Michigan Depression Center, educating people about the dangers of depression and mechanisms to deal with it. Eric lost his 15-year-old son to suicide and wants to prevent anyone else from feeling that pain.

It's really important because knowing you're not alone is a huge deal for people. Programs like this are helping former players as well. The fraternity of former NFL players is a close one, and I look at a guy like former Lions defensive back Lem Barney, who made the Hall of Fame and is suffering from early CTE. On the line and playing 18 seasons, I know I took a heck of a lot more hits than Lem. I feel pretty good right now, but I don't know what it's going to look like 18 years from now when I'm Lem's age.

But like Mike says, I signed up for it and would do it again. With football I earned more money than I would have otherwise. I made my fame and was able to provide a good life for my family, and that was not guaranteed. Think about it, I grew up in Miami and had no idea how I was ever going to get out. Even when we moved to the Brownsville sub, it was better, but there was still a lot of poverty. The choices for most folks at that time were doing construction work or going to the armed forces. Personally, I wasn't even thinking about college. Nobody in my family had gone there.

Some people live according to a plan, but I've always kind of seen what's out there and gone from there. I look back to how things have happened for me—the principal happening to see me, my trying out for football and failing. Frank Battaglia took an interest on and off the field in my development. Then all of the sudden, I'm getting scholarship offers for college.

My only goal at the University of Florida was to get my degree. Well, lo and behold, I start getting approached by agents and now I'm in the NFL.

I faltered early in my time in Detroit. It took those experiences to learn about turning the power off when I was heading back home, opening a checking account, etc. It's all part of growing up, and you have to do it in order to get where you want to be. I truly believe that everything in my life has been ordained. There were steps available in my life, and I tried to take advantage of the opportunities.

## Today's Game vs. Yesterday's Game

I love football, especially the NFL. Even in retirement I follow everything pretty closely and enjoy being associated with the league. You hear a lot of former players (in any sport) complain that today's game isn't as good as when we played. I certainly enjoyed my era, but if I were active today, I'd probably be able to play 20-plus seasons. The game has become so pass happy, and pass blocking is much easier than making holes in the running game.

One thing that does bother me a lot is that players today don't practice their craft like we used to, and that's on both sides of the ball. During my time I'd go up against guys like Reggie White, Chris Doleman, Bruce Smith, and, of course, Lawrence Taylor. It seemed like there was one lining up across from me every week. Those guys worked on their games. If I didn't match their preparation, I'd get embarrassed.

That meant things like going over my 45-degree kick step time and time again on my own after the team's practice. Even on run blocking, there were different things I had to focus on. There were no weeks off. I can tell by watching the games that guys are not working like we did. Don't get me wrong. There are a few, guys like J.J. Watt (Houston Texans), Justin Houston (Kansas City Chiefs), and Julius Peppers (Green Bay Packers).

Of course, I'm not just talking about linemen. One of my favorite teammates was Hall of Famer Aeneas Williams with the Arizona Cardinals. You could just watch him or Deion Sanders, and it's obvious they worked on their technique. Fans talk about Darrell Revis, and "Revis Island." That's not an accident. He watches all kinds of film and is the best in the NFL. The game is more about the money and the hype, but the truly great players? They have a pure love of the game, and that's why they are the best in the NFL.

## Performance-Enhancing Drugs

People ask me all the time: did I ever do steroids or other performance-enhancing drugs? I'm proud to say that the answer is NO.

To be honest I was completely ignorant to the fact that anyone was doing it for the first three or four years of my career. I guess it was out of sight, out of mind. I never needed help, but I know there were teammates who were religiously taking them. On a personal level, when I heard about all of the side effects, I was scared. Over the years, of course, there were guys doing PEDs. But when it comes to punishing guys, I always felt like that was a league thing. It made the competition unfair, but what was I supposed to do?

In my opinion, one guy who definitely used them was Kevin Fagan, who went on to win two Super Bowls with the San Francisco 49ers. When he was at the University of Miami, I just put it on him. I mean I crushed him. What do you know? The next year he put on 30 pounds, was bench pressing this, lifting that. He was a totally different guy. My attitude was, whatever. I just played with the hand I was dealt, and things turned out pretty well.

## Once a Teammate, Always a Brother

As many things that are wrong with the NFL—primarily the health concerns during and after our careers—the best part of having played in the league is the bond we all have with former teammates.

We go back further with some of these guys than we do with our spouses. Playing in a professional sport is such a rare opportunity that it's hard to find someone who can understand what you're going through at this point in your life. These guys played on the field with you. They shared sweat, blood, and tears. They were world-class athletes making a huge amount of money.

There's nothing that equals the camaraderie of being on the field with your brothers. There are good times and bad times, but you do whatever you can to play. There's a finality to your career—just like the playoffs. You'll never replace that feeling. In the NFL it's kind of like still being in college; you belong somewhere. You lose that feeling of being part of a team, and that's where real life comes in.

For players the goals are pretty simple: win a Super Bowl, make All-Pro, make a certain amount of money. But once you leave the game, all of that stuff is gone. It's easy to feel like you're just wandering around. That's hard to explain to someone that hasn't been there.

I can't speak for everyone, but I know most of us really look forward to getting together these days. Sometimes it might be a signing event, or, sadly, someone's funeral. Too many former players are dying off. I read that three to four alumni from each team pass away each year.

I will say that even when celebrating someone's life, it's really cleansing to be able to spend time with former teammates. Of course, in the case of a funeral, we're sad, but we also remember the great games, the disappointments, and the "what ifs?" Guys talk about what they're going through, whether it's physical or mental. Those guys are just like you. They were world-class professional athletes. They made millions of dollars. And then, usually somewhere in their 30s, they can no longer do the thing they love the most. Again, because we've all been to war together, we *understand* each other. It's hard to put a value on that.

## What a Championship *Will* Mean for the Lions

One nice thing about playing for a few different organizations is that it's given me a good sense of what fans around the league are like from one city to another. This is where Lions fans really stand out. When I was in New York, the Giants fans considered themselves super knowledgeable and they were. But let me tell you that here in Detroit, it's at least an even match. What makes the Lions faithful so unique in the NFL, heck, in all sports is their loyalty. They love us when we're good; they love us when we're bad. Even during some of the trials and tribulations I had as a player, the fans have given me pretty much nothing but love.

I mean, think about it. This is an organization that has won *one* playoff game since 1957! They went through an 0–16 season…and still sold out Ford Field. Fans threatened a boycott that year, but they never went through with it. There's only four teams that have never *been* to the Super Bowl, and we're one of them! We've seen former laughingstocks like the New Orleans Saints and Tampa Bay Buccaneers win championships. Even the Arizona Cardinals got to the big dance. There's nothing I'd have loved more than to be a part of the team that brings it home to Detroit. They will be immortalized. Heck, just getting there would be beyond huge.

When it happens—and it is *when*, not *if*—these guys will own not just Detroit, but the entire state of Michigan. I think back to 1991 when we were one win away from getting to the Super Bowl, and the whole state was crazy. Everyone was feeling good about themselves. Hey, word even spread to Canada because we're so close. This would be an international event!

**Barry Sanders (former Lions running back):** "There are tons of fans here, very loyal fans, most loyal in any sport. I think it would be absolute mayhem. We had a little bit of a taste of success, and I think we did sort of revive things. It's interesting that the previous year we were expected to do much more than we did and it was a little bit of a letdown. I don't think many people expected us to do much in that '91 season. So it was a pleasant surprise to go on a seven-week run. We won every home game, so it was just one of my great years—to have that type of success and win that many games in a row. If Detroit ever won a Super Bowl, it would be absolutely amazing for these fans. I think probably not much different than it was in New Orleans. For many years, for those of us who were around in the '80s and early '90s, it was hard to imagine the Saints winning anything. I think you'll see unparalleled excitement around here if that ever happens."

Look around at the city's history: when the Tigers won in 1984, unfortunately, things turned violent, but so many people celebrated the right way and were happier in their own lives. The Bad Boy Pistons may have played in Auburn Hills instead of Detroit, but they were a team for the ages. And they do call Detroit "Hockeytown" for a reason. The Red Wings have been great for so long that everyone *expects* them to win. I'm telling you, if the Lions win, it would be bigger than all of those teams *combined*!

I think this group is even closer to pulling it off than we were. You know, people don't remember, but the NFL's most successful organization, the New England Patriots, used to be a joke. They played in different home stadiums, they were sold, they almost moved several times. They had nowhere near the respect of an organization like the

Lions. Once they broke through, success bred more success. That's what will happen here.

Heading into the 2015 season, I really felt like the team was putting the pieces in place—largely thanks to the management team of Tom Lewand and Martin Mayhew. There was a totally different vibe from the Matt Millen debacle. In 2014 first-year head coach Jim Caldwell came to town and led Detroit to a surprising 11–5 record. Heck, they came within a bad call of beating the Dallas Cowboys in the NFC wild-card game. We were all ready to see the next step.

Unfortunately, you play the game on the field, and the Lions never overcame five straight losses and had to rally just to finish 7–9. Mrs. Ford said enough was enough and fired Tom and Martin.

Now, it's up to new president Ron Wood and general manager Bob Quinn to get everyone back on track. And they'll have their work cut out for them because the NFL is almost a year-to-year deal; with free agency and the salary cap, you're basically building a new team from season to another. After seeing guys like Ndamukong Suh and Nick Fairley sign with other teams and the retirement of Calvin Johnson, the new top dogs will have their hands full. But Quinn learned in New England under Bill Belichick, so maybe *this* time will work.

## My Home

Another reason I so want a championship for the Lions is because Detroit is my home. This Florida boy came to Detroit, played here for 11 seasons, bounced around a bit, and wrapped up his career with a Super Bowl title back in Florida. But why the heck am I still living in Michigan?

Well, I love living here, even though it has its challenges. During my first year with the Lions, people made a bet on whether I'd be able to navigate the snow and make it to practice on time. I remember seeing Glove's face when I woke him up at 4:30 AM because it was the first time I ever saw snow. He thought I was crazy. I actually went out and did a snow angel! And yes, I did make it to practice but not without learning all about black ice and doing two 360s on the way. Having to buy new clothes and finding out how to survive the cold was certainly a different experience.

But that change of seasons is one of the things I love. In Florida, there's hot and hotter. Here, everything changes. It's great that the state is so diverse; I mean there's every kind of person here: black, white, Hispanic, Jewish, Middle Eastern, I feel like I learn something every day. One of the biggest things that doesn't get talked about enough is how charitable people in this state are. Think about what they've been through, and it's amazing they give what they don't have.

When I came here, all I knew was that Detroit was cold, had a lot of black people, and made cars, but it's so much more. The water here is just beautiful, and everyone has a boat. It's one of the top states for golf and really all sports. And, of course, we have cars. Really, if it wasn't for Detroit, the NFL wouldn't be what it is now. When you watch a game, what types of commercials do you see the most of? Automobile commercials. Without that advertising there wouldn't be as much money spent, and it trickles down on a global level.

Right now I work in Detroit, and my group goes out and tries to find smaller companies, who are doing great work but not getting recognition. We try to connect them with bigger companies that can kind of help them get across their goal line—just like John Madden did for me when he gave recognition to the offensive linemen during his telecasts who would normally be anonymous. If you can find a small company and connect them with a bigger company, that's like scoring a touchdown. I look at it like I'm out there blocking for them, trying to find a way for some of these smaller companies to go out and work with the bigger companies.

I may have retired, but I will always be a Lion, and Detroit will always be my home.

When I was in the league, I'd always ingratiate myself with the rookies. At each stop after I left the Lions, I would never take my car up to training camp. I'd ride the bus. I was a veteran All-Pro, so it wasn't like I couldn't afford better transportation, but this was where my roots were. There would mostly be rookies on the bus—young guys who weren't going to make the team. So why did I do this? There were a couple of reasons. First, I'd get to know the guys. I've always been fascinated by people, no matter who they are, and learning about them. Also, they'd realize I was one of the guys. They'd be thinking, *Here's a guy who's been in the league 18 years, but he takes time to talk to us. He doesn't act big-time.* Whenever a boss or someone in a position of authority takes the time to bond with everyone else, it goes a long way.

That's the same approach I'm taking in business. I try to befriend the smaller companies. As a player I've been to the pinnacle, and now it's my turn to reach out and touch these companies. Everyone knows about Cleveland Cavaliers owner Dan Gilbert and hears about Quicken Loans, but nobody ever thinks they can connect with a guy like that. *Hell, he's LeBron James' boss.* This is where I come in. My goal is to be that conduit, to help connect everyone. Now don't get me wrong, the smaller companies are going to have to be qualified—I'm not bringing just anyone to my contacts—but once they are, I want to be the one to introduce them.

A lot of people are surprised to find me working in a low-profile gig like this, but let me tell you something: I'm into making quiet money. You look at ex-athletes, and they own nightclubs, restaurants, car dealerships. That's what I call "loud" money. Everyone knows you're doing well. It's the money that keeps you in the spotlight. Your name is out there. If people want to get to you, they know how to do it, and you get a lot of friends quickly. I made that loud money for

18 years during my NFL career. Now I can still do work, still affect people, connecting them with big companies, but it's in more of a quiet way.

It's all about connections. As a young player (especially an offensive lineman) in Detroit, I realized I'd have to do other things to build my name around the city. So I told the Lions that I'd do any charitable appearance, anything they needed. Of course, it came from my heart, but it also served to build my name. Soon people would know me more for what I was doing in the community, as opposed to just on the field. I had my scholarships we gave out, my foundation, which gave out money every year. I was connected with all of that stuff. One of the biggest aspects was that I stayed in the community. The first three years, I'd go back to Miami during the offseason. Then my ex-wife said, "You know, we should stay up here." I've been a Michigander ever since and proud of it.

It was a natural progression for me to go off into helping the small businessperson because I ran a couple of small businesses myself. I saw firsthand the struggles that owners would go through. The advantage I had over a lot of people was my fame, which helped me get exposure. But I knew that smaller companies wouldn't have the same advantages I did.

I have three things going for me today. I am rooted in the community, I'm a local celebrity, and I know the struggle of the small business owner. That all sort of pushed me in that direction. What really got me into the diversity area was Dan Gilbert. Dan is a huge entrepreneur and Detroit real estate investor. One of his companies brought me in to start learning the business side of things.

**Dan Gilbert (Rock Ventures and Quicken Loans founder and chairman)**: "I met Lomas in 2005 through a mutual friend and business partner. Lomas expressed a strong desire to learn and grow his business knowledge, and I saw this as an opportunity to mentor a hardworking go-getter in his business pursuits after his NFL career. I was a big fan of him during his tenure with the Detroit Lions and saw connecting with him as an opportunity to get him more involved in and around the Detroit community, where he spent 11 seasons. Lomas is a very personable guy with a great ability to build relationships very quickly. He has always been very engaged in our conversations and his work with our family of companies. Lomas is curious and insightful. He asks thoughtful questions in every meeting and discussion. Most of all he is a great cultural fit: a roll-up-his-sleeves, hardworking, blue-collar guy. Not only does he take care of the blocking and tackling, but he also has the capacity and skill to create and innovate."

For the past couple of years, they've been training me on the procedures, processes, and such. This involves workforce, which includes hiring people but also being a supplier. That means finding small companies to connect with one of Dan's companies. For example, when he needed someone to clean his offices, I would find a smaller, minority-owned janitorial company that could handle cleaning that size building. I'll vet that company, make sure they're certified, and then I would take that company back to Title Source (Dan's company) and introduce them. On top of that, it's a minority-owned company, so it helps promote diversity.

**Gilbert**: "Outside of mentoring Lomas and his business pursuits, we connected him with key business leaders from our family of companies to help him learn, grow, and even get involved directly with the operations of those businesses. The most essential message that we stressed to him was the importance of culture in business. Culture is everything and, in my humble opinion, businesses, teams, and organizations live or die by the culture and environments they create."

The car industry is a good example of why diversity is important. A lot of cars go for between $20,000 to $30,000. The average income in our country is around $25,000. So when you have suppliers who have some skin in the game—like the people who make the tires—they're more likely to buy your product. They need to include blacks, women, all minorities because everyone buys a car. The wealth has to be spread. If the cars are too expensive and people can't afford them, companies are going to out of business. Suppliers need to be diverse, and Detroit is the mecca of diversity.

The people here are so welcoming. And they *love* their holidays. In Florida they celebrate the holidays, but it's hard to get into the Christmas spirit when it's 70 degrees out. Do you know that I never heard of a paczki, a delicious Polish pastry, until I moved here? If you haven't had one, you have no idea what you're missing. In November and December, you see houses lit up to celebrate. It wasn't like that down South.

Detroit also happens to be one of the best sports cities in America. I've been able to take advantage of that, too, meeting guys like former Red Wings stars Steve Yzerman and Sergei Fedorov; ex-Pistons greats Joe Dumars, Isiah Thomas, and Vinnie Johnson; and Tigers legends Cecil Fielder, Willie Horton, and Denny McLain.

Obviously, being a successful athlete anywhere has its perks, and that's been the case for me. I was fortunate enough to meet Coleman Young, the first black mayor of Detroit, and that was a tremendous thrill. I know there were some haters out there, but this dude was awesome.

It's the story of my life. I never figured something like that would happen to me, never thought I'd live in Michigan, but I'm here and I love it.

# ACKNOWLEDGMENTS

The process of summing up an 18-year NFL career—an entire life for that matter—can be overwhelming. I agreed to the project but really had no idea what to expect. But I'll tell you what, it was therapeutic. There were difficult times, but overall, it was a blast.

It's incredible to me how much goes into writing a book. It's almost like a football gameplan; there's an outline that provides the direction you want to go, but you've got to be able to improvise, too. It seems like every time that Mike would sit down—either with me or with any of his interviews—he'd come up with a nugget, and the next thing we knew, we had a whole new chapter.

I want to thank all of my friends, teammates, and family members who were so generous with their time. I'm sure I'll forget someone, but it's not on purpose.

My former coaches were a big part of my success and of this book. Thanks to Wayne Fontes, who is so underrated it's ridiculous. Wayne is the best coach in recent Lions history, there's no doubt. My old line coach with the Lions and Bucs—Bill Muir, who I can never repay for sharing his knowledge. Jon Gruden brought me home to Tampa and got me my Super Bowl ring. Coach, I can call myself a champion because of you. And, while he's not a coach, Bill Keenist has been in charge of media relations for the Lions forever. He was a huge help on and off the field.

Then there were the guys I lined up with, starting with the guy I've known the longest, Kevin Glover. Glove and I met at the 1985 Senior Bowl and have been boys ever since. He didn't get as many accolades as he should have in the pros, but I'm so proud of him getting into the University of Maryland Hall of Fame in 2015.

I don't think I ever played with anyone who loved football more than Chris Spielman. This was a guy who tackled his grandmother! The stories are all true, and thank you, Chris, for sharing them. A hell of a linebacker, but an even better husband, father, and man. It's an honor to call him a friend.

When I met Mike Utley, he was the grunge-looking dude, who thought he was hot stuff. I'm proud of the football player he became, but I'm even more proud of how he took a life-altering accident and turned it into an inspiring story of perseverance. Thumbs up, and congrats on being inducted into the College Football Hall of Fame!

Rob Rubick had no business making it in the NFL as a 12th-round draft pick out of Grand Valley State. *They don't even have a 12th round anymore.* But Rubes played six years and continues to be Mr. Lion, in good times and bad.

But, of course, when you're talking about great Lions, the list starts with Barry Sanders. When he came into the league, B was like Bambi in the woods—quiet and wide-eyed. He spent so much time at my house that we actually thought about legally adopting him. One of the most fun parts of putting this book together was thinking about B hanging with my daughters—not as the greatest running back ever—but just a kid chilling with other kids. Barry did his best to eat everything we had, but it was our pleasure. I always had his back on the field and will always do the same off of it.

As much as I enjoyed *playing* the game, I think I've liked talking about it just as much. There have been so many media members who spent countless hours mentoring me in the business. I'll forever be thankful and appreciate their input on this project. Dana Jacobson, Jay Crawford, and Rob Parker, you guys are the best.

Then there's my family. My sister, Valerie Bradley, was a treasure trove of great information for Mike to tap in to. Through the ups and downs, we're always family, and I'll always love you, Val.

When recalling more than 52 years of stories, I know sometimes my details were a bit fuzzy. Mike really counted on Football-reference. com to double-check. He also did research, using back issues of publications such as *Sports Illustrated*.

The heart of this book came from Mike talking to the folks I mentioned, and I thank all of them.